"In this series of intimate and luminous reflections, annual letters to a godson, Stanley Hauerwas lifts up a rich array of virtues. He does so not in order to exhort their cultivation but to display how they ride on the back of compelling practices and forms of life that we discover along the way."

— JENNIFER A. HERDT
Yale Divinity School

"Emerson thought that achieving aversion from conformity might require the enabling attentiveness of an older friend. These letters show how a godparent can embody the same emancipatory, upbuilding aspirations in a distinctively Christian idiom, exhibiting exactly the virtues that it sets itself to discuss."

— STEPHEN MULHALL
New College, Oxford

"I think I'm supposed to say that this book shows 'a gentler side of Stanley.' But as far as I am concerned, there was never any other. Typically, for Hauerwas, it combines theoretical exposition with a direct, interpersonal context. . . . What we have here is an exemplary short summa of the practical Christian virtues in the form of an enactment of the crucial virtue of godparenthood."

— JOHN MILBANK
University of Nottingham

"This is an invaluable, one-off book in both form and content. . . . A central insight is that our virtues are pulled out of us by our loves—pets, games, politics included, all explored with abundant humility, humor, and passion."

— ANN LOADES
Durham University

The Character of Virtue

Letters to a Godson

STANLEY HAUERWAS
with an Introduction by Samuel Wells

WILLIAM B. EERDMANS PUBLISHING COMPANY
GRAND RAPIDS, MICHIGAN

Wm. B. Eerdmans Publishing Co.
2140 Oak Industrial Drive NE, Grand Rapids, Michigan 49505
www.eerdmans.com

27 26 25 24 23 22 21 20 19 18   1 2 3 4 5 6 7 8 9 10

ISBN 978-0-8028-7579-2

Library of Congress Cataloging-in-Publication Data

Names: Hauerwas, Stanley, 1940– author.
Title: The character of virtue : letters to a godson /
    Stanley Hauerwas ; with an introduction by Samuel Wells.
Description: Grand Rapids : Eerdmans Publishing Co., 2018.
Identifiers: LCCN 2017054356 |
    ISBN 9780802875792 (hardcover : alk. paper)
Subjects: LCSH: Character. | Virtue. | Virtues. |
    Hauerwas, Stanley, 1940—Correspondence.
Classification: LCC BJ1531 .H38 2018 | DDC 241/.4—dc23
    LC record available at https://lccn.loc.gov/2017054356

Contents

Contents

On Being a Godparent

WHAT A GODPARENT IS

The term "godparent" has two kinds of largely unhelpful connotations. The first is gothic and sometimes rather terrifying. Francis Ford Coppola's 1972 film *The Godfather* tells the story of how Michael Corleone emerges from the shadows as his father's youngest son and becomes the ruthless leader of a murderous mafia clan. It teaches the viewer never to trust a man holding a violin case, and to associate the term "godparent" with manipulation, violence, and virulent lust for power. Meanwhile, in Pyotr Ilyich Tchaikovsky's 1892 ballet *The Nutcracker*, based on E. T. A. Hoffmann's story, the children of the house gather round the sparkling Christmas tree, whereupon, as the clock strikes eight, in walks the mysterious Herr Drosselmeyer, councilor, magician, and godfather to the daughter of the house, Clara. He brings with him four dancing dolls, made by his own hand, and a wooden nutcracker in the form of a diminutive man, whose midnight transformation into a life-size character drives the rest of the story. The ballet teaches the viewer to see a godparent as a purveyor of mysteries, fables, and magical dreams. Then there's the 1697 Charles Perrault fairy tale *Cinderella*, which tells how a young woman, though oppressed by her stepsisters and forced into virtual slavery, nonetheless goes to the Prince's ball and wins his heart through the intervention of her Fairy Godmother, who conjures dress, slippers, carriage, and footmen with nonchalant aplomb. This tale teaches that a godparent can make dreams come true, especially for those in the gutter.

If these historic connotations of a godparent are unduly vivid, the contemporary alternative is invariably anodyne. Faced with an upcoming baptism, parents cast around anxiously for suitable friends or family members who may be relied upon to take seriously the threefold challenge of being conversant with Christianity, representing a not-entirely-inappropriate role model, and remembering to send Christmas and birthday presents without undue prompting. Those in receipt of such an invitation divide between the honored, conscientious, prayerful, and attentive, and the dilatory, sheepish, and neglectful. But to be fair to the latter (probably the large majority), there is minimal support for the task. Who teaches you what it means to be a godparent?

Where are the how-to guides, the godparenthood-for-dummies manuals, the confessions-of-a-lapsed-godparent tell-all memoirs? A quick Google search on "being a godparent" reveals a majority of entries deliberating conscientiously about whether one can be a godparent if one is not a Christian. There are undoubtedly a series of exceptions; but there seems to be no rule.

In an early essay, Stanley Hauerwas points out that the origin of "gossip" is *god-sibb*—the conversation of close friends and family members in considering the well-being of a younger member of the household. Today we think of gossip as always a bad thing—the discussion of the interests and actions of third parties without true regard to profound goods like loyalty, trust, confidentiality, empathy, and compassion; the trading of others' secrets for the betterment of one's own reputation as a lively conversationalist. But gossip began among the inner circle of those whose judgment was genuinely sought out, whose kindly spirit was beyond question, and whose concern was genuine.

A godparent is one who stays faithful to God, and faithful to their godchild, and seeks regular conversation with the one about the other—godly *god-sibb*, habitual interchange about how we may walk in God's ways, and about how, as we walk our ways, we find God walking beside us. This book is intended to be a practical companion for godparents, taking up themes as they arise in the life of godchild and godparent, and trusting that in the relationship between the two the ways of God will surface and the purposes of God will become clear. A godparent doesn't so much guide the godchild through the contours of life or make crucial interventions at moments of decision; instead, the godparent remains faithful whatever the contours of life and abides even when the decisions have mostly been bad ones. This is a book about such faithfulness and such abiding.

What a Godparent Can Be

I have nine godchildren. When I was young and single and had fewer responsibilities for others, I was a much more assiduous and attentive godparent—certainly in the active role model and reliable birthday-rememberer categories—than I am now. On one occasion I was asked to preach at a godchild's baptism, and what I said then, I addressed also to myself (in *God's Companions*, chap. 5):

We have gathered together for a precious and holy moment. We shall shortly be re-enacting the first public moment of Jesus' ministry. And just as we believe God is especially present when we re-enact Jesus' last meal with his disciples, so we believe he is especially present when we re-enact his baptism in the Jordan. What happens at baptism is that God places a song in your heart. But it is very important that there are other people present—because it is very easy, especially when you are less than four months old, to forget the tune. So you have godparents. It is up to the godparent to learn the song so well that they can sing it back to you when you forget how it goes. (See Bausch, *Telling Stories, Compelling Stories*, 1991, 171–72.) So, listen carefully, godparents: we're relying on you.

And what is the song? Well, the story of Jesus' baptism shows us what the song is. Three things happen in this story. The heavens open; the Spirit descends like a dove; and a voice says "This is my beloved child." Each of these events has great significance.

The beginning of the song goes like this: *Heaven is open to you.* (See Bruner, *The Christbook*, 1987, 83–94.) Look at what happens in the story of Jesus: the Gospel begins with the tearing of the heavens and ends with the tearing of the temple curtain. The veil between you and God has been torn apart. Heaven is open to you. There is no limit to God's purpose for your life: it is an eternal purpose.

Now you may find that your godparents sidle up to you when you are making a choice of career: they may say, "Don't dive for cover, don't just do what your parents did or want: *heaven* is open to you. The sky isn't the limit: there is no limit." Or if a time comes when you are facing serious illness, even death, your godparents, knowing the song in your heart, may say: "The angels are waiting for you, they know you by name: heaven is *open* to you. Death is the gate to the open heaven."

And the second line of the song goes like this: *God's Spirit is in you.* Remember the end of [the story of] the flood, when the dove brought the twig of new life back to Noah? Well, here is the dove descending on Jesus, bringing the gift of the Holy Spirit. [The gift implies] you are now the Temple of God's Holy Spirit. You are the place where others will encounter God. God's Spirit is in you.

If a time comes in your life when you feel alone and surrounded by hostility, you may hear a godparent gently whispering a tune: "You may feel evil is all around you, but you can still worship, for God's *Spirit* is in you." Or if a time comes when you are wildly successful, you may hear a sterner song: "*God's* Spirit is in you—everyone may worship you, but don't forget whom *you* worship." You may be cross with your godparent at the time, but they may be singing the song in your heart, and reminding you of your baptism.

So, heaven is open to you; God's Spirit is in you; and finally, the third line of the song of baptism: *You mean everything to God.* God's words are "This is my beloved Son." These words mean, "Jesus means everything to God, and everything God gives to Jesus he gives to us." You mean everything to God.

There may come a time in your life when you feel a deep sense of [your own missing the mark,] of your own sin. Then you should hear your godparent say, "You are everything to *God*. You still are, whatever you have done, however unworthy you feel." Or you may wander away from the Church because God seems so distantly cosmic and ethereally vague, when you long for intimacy and passion. Then you may hear your godparents sing, through their tears, "You are *everything* to God. Remember your song."

So, this is what baptism is: God places a song in your heart. And so your godparents' role is this: to learn that song so well that they can sing it back to you when you forget how it goes. And this is the song: "Heaven is open to you; God's Spirit is in you; you are everything to God." This is the song that makes your heart sing. And what does the song mean? I'll tell you. You are the song in God's heart, and he will never forget how you go.

A godparent is a companion—literally, one who shares bread—with growing child, with parent, and with God. Each relationship has its own integrity. A growing child has very few adults in her life to whom she is not connected by familial ties or contractual expectations. The flaw in the former is that they are permanent and inescapable, however problematic and distressing they may sometimes be. The flaw in the latter—the dance teacher, the school nurse—is that they are appropriately boundaried and invariably short-term. A godparent fills the gap between the two: he or she has the potential intimacy of the former and the option of less frequent contact should the relationship not prove life-giving. In an ideal scenario the godparent carries out a genuinely priestly role: representing God to the growing child in constancy, listening, understanding, and love; and representing the growing child to God in intercession, thanksgiving, and sometimes lament.

A relationship between godparent and parent is, at its best, one of critical friend. The godparent loves both growing child and parent, and represents, on occasion, the one to the other. "I've noticed you're reading her text messages; it seems like the trust between you has got to a difficult place" is the caring, nonjudgmental observation of a critical friend. "I get the feeling you're finding it hard to talk with your parents about the things that really matter" is a similar such observation. Such *god-sibb* opens the door that a parent or growing child may be longing to walk through for understanding, solidarity, space to reflect, or gentle challenge. The godparent is the ideal person with whom the parent can discuss the growing child's spiritual development—whether she doesn't like attending church anymore, or whether, when we all light a candle and try for a few moments to be quiet together at the end of the day, she insists on blowing the candle out. Such issues don't have simple solutions. The point for the godparent is not to fix the problem, but to dwell in the place of discernment with sympathy and grace.

The godparent is the one who asks the second question. The first question is (to the parent), "How's my precious goddaughter doing?"—to which the answer may be a list of school reports and clashes with siblings and ratings of grandparent-satisfaction and tidiness of bedroom. The second question is simply, "How's she really doing?" In the hurly-burly of life, even the first question can easily go unaddressed.

And the godparent may be the only person who ever asks the second question. Likewise, when the same question is addressed to the growing child, the first answer may be a litany of dance classes, school clubs, upcoming tests, broken friendships, and tryouts for one team or another. From an early age the growing child may have learned that these are the signposts by which an adult navigates the mysteries of a young person's emerging existence. That young person may never have been asked the second question. It may be so strange that they can't initially grasp how it's different from the first question. But over time they may come to realize that, while the first question is the one that dominates their world, the second question is the one God cares about.

Michael Ramsey once called priests to be "with God, with people on your hearts." That names the priestly role of the godparent—to be with God, with their godchild on their heart, and to be with their godchild, with God on their heart. It is a role both daunting and simple. The daunting part is to recognize that getting involved in the work of the Holy Spirit is likely to change all involved. The simple part is that it's the Holy Spirit that does all the real work: one only has to be willing to participate.

On Being a Godparent

A GODPARENT CALLED STANLEY

For obvious reasons, when parents seek out godparents for their child, they begin by considering their friends. By the time my first child, Laurence, was born in June 2002, Stanley Hauerwas had become my friend. After I completed my formal ministerial training, including a degree in systematic theology, in 1991, I explored ways to deepen my understanding of what a holy life might genuinely mean for a layperson. (If I was to be a helpful pastor, it was high time I found out.) I had already begun to read the extensive writings of Stanley Hauerwas, and found his work uniquely helpful in bringing together the deepest questions of theology with the longing to express them within the life of the church. He was known for his writing in ethics, but I quickly realized the conventional theological silos of Bible, history, theology, philosophy, ethics, and pastoral studies were of no interest to him. His restlessness resonated with my sense that Jesus came to unsettle, rather than to comfort, and the angles from which he addressed the issues of today and forever intrigued and challenged me to a degree I hadn't found in any other contemporary theological writing. He was, in short, talking about the questions I was asking, with a fearless relish that I longed to imitate.

We met in late 1991—an occasion of which he retains no memory: I found a person whose Texan accent I could scarcely understand, whose shambling walk made me dance to keep step, whose piercing gaze told me he was really serious, and the glint in whose eye told me that despite his utter seriousness, he was also ready to play. As one who grew up in England, I, of course, didn't have an accent. But I knew I was serious and I was certainly longing to play—and twenty-six years later I realize that this combination of restless inquiry and playful companionship has characterized everything that we've shared.

I started to send him things I was working on and subjected myself to the (still daunting) challenge of reading his handwriting. We met and spoke together at conferences and got to know one another's wives. Then Stanley was asked to deliver the Gifford Lectures at St. Andrews in 2001, and I traveled to Scotland to spend a few days with him and hear the first two lectures. Together we climbed a Munro—one of the 282 mountains in Scotland with a height of over 3,000 feet—and somewhere on the way up or down we became friends. C. S. Lewis speaks of the moment two raindrops on a windowpane coalesce and become one, and hasten downwards all the faster: that was what happened after that day. Shortly afterwards we began to write a book together, and in the writing of that book I realized serious theology was no longer a hobby for me: I now had a dual vocation to be a theologically formed pastor and an ecclesially shaped writer—a vocation different from Stanley's, but one that he understood and encouraged more than anyone.

And so, when Jo and I had our first child, it seemed obvious to us to ask Stanley to be his godfather. We were under no illusions about the Christmas-and-birthday-present purchasing. I simply wanted my son to enter into the companionship and critical friendship that I had experienced and that I trusted (rightly, as it turned out) would long continue. Since we lived 4,000 miles apart, I suggested Stanley exercise his godparental ministry in a way that to most people would be demanding and unreasonable but to him was natural and appropriate: by writing Laurie a letter to mark his baptism, and by writing each subsequent year on the anniversary, each time focusing on a particular virtue that seemed suitable for his stage in life, until Laurie was old enough to read them for himself.

Over the next three years, that was exactly what happened, and, bringing great joy, each year Stanley and his wife, Paula, would find an occasion to be in England and visit Laurie to incarnate the sentiments expressed in the letter. But then an unexpected thing came to pass. Jo and I were invited to take up appointments at Duke University, and the whole household, by now including a young sister, Stephanie, upped and moved to North Carolina. This was no longer a relationship of phone calls and letters and the occasional visit. This was now an almost daily interaction of scholarly collaboration, serious and playful conversation, shared worship, bedtime stories, baseball and basketball. Stanley's rule of life ran closely alongside the Book of Common Prayer, but was just as closely tied to hot Mexican meals, Durham Bulls evenings, and spare tickets for the Blue Devils basketball tyros in Cameron Indoor Stadium. If Laurie was to be a godson, he needed to be inducted into these various halls of fame.

And so the letters changed, from speculative imaginings from a distant shore to well-informed counsel from an incarnate godfather, whose *god-sipp* was truly based on shared discernment with parents, and just occasionally on being a refuge from parents who didn't always grasp the necessity of one more bedtime story. On October 27 each year, we would try to create an opportunity for Laurie to come to the Divinity School and ascend the three flights of stairs that led him to Stanley's office, so he could receive his letter—in truth, as welcome to him as five beans were to Jack's mother in the beanstalk story.

Great was the grief when in 2012 the sojourn in Durham drew to a close, and all parties returned to the status quo ante 2005. But some things never change. Aristotle says, "Give me a child until he is seven and I will show you the man," and, after seven years of this child and this man living in close proximity, the letters were by now based on an understanding between godparent and godson that less frequent contact was not going to shake.

STANLEY AS A GODPARENT

What do the letters actually say? Each letter picks out a virtue as particularly suitable for Laurie to contemplate as he enters the next year of his emerging life. There are four cardinal and three theological virtues, seven in all—prudence, justice, temperance, fortitude, faith, hope, and love.

Virtue matters because it enables us to realize our potential. Virtue names the ways good habits become inscribed on our character by steering between excess and defect. Christopher Robin put things much the same way in his song "Halfway up the Stairs." Aristotle and A. A. Milne are on the same page. For Aristotle, having too much of something is as bad as not having enough. Too much self-confidence results in rashness; too little results in fear. Courage names the right balance between fear and rashness. Aristotle calls this right balance the mean. To take another example, pleasure is one extreme and pain is another. The name of the mean between pleasure and pain is temperance. Like Goldilocks, Aristotle was looking for porridge that was not too hot, not too cold, but just right. All the virtues lie halfway up the stairs—"not up, not down," not in the nursery and not in the town.

So while there are seven virtues, there should be fourteen vices, because the vices are the extremes that the virtues lie between. Those who are struggling with a sin are generally at the bottom of a staircase the top end of which is also unhealthy; but in between lies the thing they're looking for. Thus, if they're feeling trodden on like a doormat, the alternative is not for them to be doing all the treading, but to restore some kind of balance of power in their relationships which today tends to be called assertiveness. If they're struggling with lust, the answer isn't simply to shut down physically or sensually but to discover forms of touch that aren't sexual and forms of sexuality that aren't all about touch. If they're struggling with doubt, the answer isn't to leap into fanaticism but to try to practice something in between called faith.

To take another example, consider the alternative vices of hyperactivity and sloth. In Luke 12, Jesus says, "Are not five sparrows sold for two pennies? Yet not one of them is forgotten in God's sight. But even the hairs of your head are all counted. Do not be afraid; you are of more value than many sparrows." In Matthew 6, Jesus says, "Look at the birds of the air; they neither sow nor reap nor gather into barns, and yet your heavenly Father feeds them. Are you not of more value than they?"

Jesus encourages us to value things for their own sake. The slothful person only values things as a means to an end: to escape the dreariness or insignificance of life. Unless something is the best, or secures astonishing excellence or wild applause, it's no more than a thudding reminder of our mundane humanity. The hyperactive person values nothing, for fear that the time taken to enjoy it might diminish the having or gaining or doing of something else. The mean between sloth and hyperactivity is peace. Peace not with others but with yourself—with your own humanity. You are not God. You will not live forever, unless God chooses to invite you to do so. You are not perfect. You are not superhuman. And yet God loves you as you are, enjoys you as you are, shapes his whole life to be in relationship with you in Jesus, and is interested in you not as a means to any end but for your own sake.

Every time you appreciate a person in their unique humanity, embark on an activity that takes every ounce of your concentration, or dwell on an aspect of the natural or human creation for its own sake, you are living halfway up the stairs between hyperactivity and sloth. At the root of both hyperactivity and sloth is fear, and its consequent impulse is either not to bother or to race maniacally, the response of fight or flight. The answer sometimes is to stay still and pay attention, to do one thing and do it well.

This is the logic of what Stanley says to Laurie about his emerging life. Virtue is the mean between two vices. In each of these letters, Stanley identifies a virtue and then sets it in context by exploring the personal and social vices and temptations between which it steers. In his baptism letter he says, "I'll try very hard never to lie to you"—and this undertakes to steer away from a rose-tinted portrayal of the Christian life. Accordingly, he identifies what went wrong for many Christians in the twentieth century: "They sought unconsciously to be as free as possible from suffering and as a result lost their ability to live as Christians." He also defines his role: "The traditional role of the godparent is to tell you the stories of the faith and in particular the stories of the church into which you were baptized, and then to tell back to that church the stories of your life.

That's the way the church is built up in holiness." And he sets out the purpose of virtue: "Christians lead lives that would be unintelligible if God wasn't present to us through the life, death, and resurrection of Jesus Christ." Finally, he offers words that crystallize the story told in this introduction: "In a world that believes time is in short supply, God has given us all the time we need to become friends with one another. And in becoming friends with each other, we learn to become friends with God. I hope you will come to count me as a friend."

In his first anniversary letter, Stanley sets the tone for all the letters that follow. He believes kindness is "the very character of God." But he is well aware that kindness is problematic for children, because "Children know they have needs, and they want their needs to be met immediately. For this reason, they sometimes don't recognize that others also have needs to be met." In words that epitomize the way these letters distill both centuries of theology and decades of personal reflection, he notes, "The greatest threat to our being virtuous usually comes not from vice but from dispositions that are similar to virtue. The great enemy of kindness, for example, is sentimentality." But with an eye to the life his godson is living, he takes a moment to establish what it means to be kind in the context of having a golden retriever as a pet.

In his next letter, on truthfulness, Stanley acknowledges the degree to which his Christian ethic is also a Texan ethic. Texans, he admits, "often confuse candor and truthfulness." But just as his counsel is rooted in self-knowledge, so he exhibits close observation of his godson on his occasional visits. "Notice, for example, how you acquired and lost power as you learned to speak. As long as you pointed to what you wanted, you had your mom and dad under your control. They had to guess what you wanted or what would satisfy you. But when you learned to name things, you lost power, because now you could be reasoned with."

The tone changes in the following letter, as Stanley begins to imagine Laurie moving to Durham, North Carolina, and the relationship changing significantly. He is unsentimental about what Laurie is leaving behind: "There is a nastiness to the Brits that can be quite attractive when contrasted to the American demand to be nice at all times." And he thinks it's time to introduce Laurie to the sober reality "that Americans in the past slaughtered Native Americans, and that we were a slave-holding nation." And, in what could be an epitaph for the whole book, Stanley declares, "Aristotle thought friendship between old people (and I am an old person) and young people was impossible because the difference in ages just made them too dissimilar. He would have thought that you and I don't have enough in common to be friends. We may well find these judgments severe, but we must also acknowledge that whether we like it or not, what Aristotle has to say about the difficulty of true friendship is unfortunately often the case—unless we are Christians."

Now the letters become more personal and more grounded in direct interaction. But they still arise from both theological and self-reflective wisdom. "Many, quite understandably, find me tiresome to be around," Stanley freely acknowledges as he describes the contrast between patience and anger. He draws on his own childhood to induct Laurie into what it means to be an apprentice in virtue. Crucial to that quest is to recognize that growing up in Christ is a team game: "The virtues aren't recommendations for individual achievement. The truth is that we can be patient only through being made patient through the patient love of others."

When Laurie is only five years old, already Stanley is beginning to talk with him about death. (These letters are not about shielding a godson from the truth.) That enables him to say, "Hope is the virtue that takes pleasure in our need for others." Laurie is being inducted into a community of faith. By the age of six, Laurie is learning about justice: "America is a social order based on the assumption that the task of political institutions is to secure agreements between people who share little in common other than the fear of death. That's why many Americans presume that a just society can be achieved without the people who make that society just." It's as well Laurie has already learned that his godfather has a seriousness of gaze but a twinkle in his eye. Yet there are uncompromising things that must be said: "Justice born of love demands that the unjust be treated justly. . . . To kill in the name of justice means such a justice cannot be the justice of God." The letters also take note of the national and local environment in which Laurie is growing up. Stanley mentions Barack Obama's election as president; he also draws in some of Laurie's father's own theological writing to emphasize what it means that "courage is required in our everyday interactions."

Basketball and baseball are inevitably drawn into the practical illustration of embodying virtue. "You're being raised in a world of privilege," Stanley points out. "The strong, the intelligent, the well-off, and the noble make up your everyday world." Stanley responds to this with his deep knowledge of the life of a bricklayer and the realities of what it means to be developmentally disabled.

And then the tone changes once more, with Laurie's move back to London. "It was a sad going. You and your family have gone back to England. . . . I'll miss taking you to see Duke basketball games." In a somber mood, Stanley perceives truths few would dare to name: "Constancy . . . means you can't let envy or resentment determine your life. If they do, then constancy has been displaced by the desire to be 'known.' Of course, it's a good thing to be known and loved by others. But when the desire to be known becomes an attempt to avoid loneliness, it can undermine constancy insofar as it often leads to desperation. When we become desperate, we can be sure we've forgotten who (and whose) we are."

Stanley's contact with Laurie becomes inevitably less regular, and his perceptions become accordingly more general: "I have a sense that those who are young float on a sea of desires." Stanley, too, is in transition: "I've been retired now for two years, but I can't seem to get the hang of it." And loss weighs heavier than before: "It's been a good year, but the death of Eden, our eighteen-year-old cat, made Paula and me very sad." All reflection arises from context. In another line that could sum up the book, Stanley comments, "I'm proposing that you think of generosity as the capacity to participate imaginatively in the experience, the life, of others." Finally, Stanley concludes the letters with an account of character. He admits "the embarrassing fact that it is by no means clear that we know what we're talking about when we praise someone for having character." But any reader of this book will by now have realized that what is meant by character is all that is contained in the pages already turned.

THE CHARACTER OF VIRTUE

The last thing to say by way of introduction is to explain, briefly, what triggered the writing of these letters and how these letters reflect this larger narrative.

Stanley is an angry, happy man and a happy, angry man. What makes him angry is to see the way, particularly in the United States, Christianity has been transposed into a benign form of therapy or a soundtrack for nationalist ideology, and, in particular, the way that project has been underwritten by some of America's most famous and distinguished theologians. Just as the twentieth-century Swiss theologian Karl Barth lamented how his German mentors had lost their credibility by supporting the Kaiser in the First World War, so Stanley has repeatedly denounced his contemporaries and forebears (both liberal and conservative) for making the church invisible by equating it with America or by collapsing the faith into a form of self-help.

This anger turns constructive when Stanley seeks to identify, first, on what ground the church's faith should instead stand, and second, how the church forms the character of its members. In regard to the church's faith, he speaks in his early career of vision, and how Christianity teaches its adherents to learn to see the world truthfully. Later he speaks more extensively of narrative—the way Christians, in baptism, move from a story which they choose to a story which they inherit. That is, to be a Christian is to discover you are a part of a whole set of stories, of which the Bible provides the definitive shape. The moment when/where Christians learn those stories is, most of all, in worship. In worship those stories are turned into practices, like being reconciled and sharing food, and these practices shape the imagination. The church forms the character of its members most of all through worship, which shapes the imagination of a congregation in such a way that its members perceive the ways of God.

These two broad themes—the distinctiveness and narrative shape of Christian convictions, and the process by which character is formed—become the signature tunes of Stanley's theology. He reads and converses across an enormous spectrum. He gives detailed attention to developmental disability and makes close observation of dying children. He offers sophisticated analyses of contemporary politics and absorbing treatments of conventional ethical subjects. His work is a vast canvas of arguments, disputes, proposals, and dialogues. But the decisive move comes in the early 1980s, when he commits himself to nonviolence as the faithful interpretation of the narrative of Jesus. For him, theology is no longer the attempt to reconcile the claims of faith with the facts of science. He shows how the death and resurrection of Jesus, with their corresponding parameters of forgiveness and eternal life, are truly the "grain of the universe," and how faith means working with that grain. The one question people love to ask him is how his bold advocacy of God's peaceable kingdom sits alongside his sometimes abrasive and plain-speaking public persona.

By now it should be clear how the themes of this book resonate with the endeavors and energies of Stanley's theological career. By schooling one growing child in the virtues, Stanley is giving detailed attention to formation, just as his own father gave such detailed attention to teaching him, as a young apprentice, to lay brick. By inducting one growing child into the narrative of the church (set amid competing and overlapping narratives of Texas, basketball, the American South, nationalism, and contemporary adolescence), he is seeking to show how faith is not fundamentally a choice, but an allowing of the self to be clothed with the stories of salvation and the saints. In short, he is as a godparent practicing what, as a theologian, he has preached.

The book that Stanley and I wrote together was, in some ways, the culmination of his career, and in other ways the beginning of mine. In this book we brought colleagues together to articulate the nature of Christian life and to describe how that life was shaped and characterized by participating in the Eucharist. On the night before he died, Jesus faced the question of how his followers could both imitate his path and meanwhile stay together. His command was "Eat together." In eating together they would discover what it would take to gather, to become one, to confess their failings, to be forgiven, to praise, to remember their story, to realize where God was at work among them, to declare their faith, to make intercession, to share peace and be reconciled with one another, to give thanks, to share, to ensure nothing is wasted, to be blessed and sent out in mission: in short, to be the church. In other words, worship is a training in virtue for head, hand, heart, and soul. If you want to discover how to be a godparent, let your imagination be shaped in virtue by worship.

In my life I have faced different personal, ministerial, and missionary challenges from Stanley, but like him, I have tried to ground my reasoning on my trust in the sufficiency of what the Holy Spirit gives the church to address all that challenges and promises to renew it. Other books I've written since our collaboration have been explorations of Christian faith that began in response to various life contexts rather different from Stanley's, but generated through wisdom learned from and invariably conversations had with Stanley, leading in directions compatible with yet often contrasting with trajectories on which Stanley himself had journeyed. Such is companionship in the gospel.

I have never been Stanley's student; I have been privileged to be his friend, collaborator, companion, and grateful critic. This book began because I wanted to say, "Stanley—you've been like a godfather to me, and allowed me to become a kind of godbrother. Now, will you do something I don't know how to do—be a godfather to my son?" What has resulted is, I believe, an insight into the heart of growing up, the heart of sharing faith, the heart of Stanley—and the heart of God.

Samuel Wells

THE LETTERS

For
Laurence Bailey Wells
on His Baptism

= *October 27, 2002* =

Dear Laurie,

I'm honored to be asked to be to be your godfather.
I'm sorry I wasn't able to witness your baptism, but
I couldn't get there from North Carolina. I live far
away, but that I can still be your godfather is a sign
that helps us understand what we do as a church in
your baptism. God makes us members of his Christ
through baptism, which means national boundaries
can't determine our relations to one another. So even
though I'm many miles away from the place where
you have been baptized, God makes it possible for us
to be present to one another through prayer. Please

know that on the wonderful day of your baptism, you are in my prayers.

I confess I find it frightening to be asked to be your godfather. It tempts me to be more than I am. We live in desperate times, particularly desperate for Christians. The church has lost its political and social power and is increasingly losing its power to form the lives of even those who want to be Christian. I very much want to be Christian, but it's an ongoing process which I'm quite sure I will never get right. So I'm tempted to try to be more wise than I am, because I want you to find being Christian a wonderful, life-giving way of life.

But for me to pretend to be wise would be pretentious. And there's nothing I hate more in life than pretension. I'm originally from Texas, and Texans are people who have had their pretensions ground into the ground by the hard land we found we couldn't master. Texans, in short, are people who have nothing to live up to. What you see is what you get.

So as your godfather all I can promise is that I'll try very hard never to lie to you. That's a difficult assignment—not because I might want to lie, but because so often our lives are constituted by lies we barely recognize. Through your baptism, God makes you part of a people vulnerable to the truth. The traditional role of the godparent is to tell you the stories of the faith and in particular the stories of the church into which you were baptized, and then to tell back to that church the stories of your life. That's the way the church is built up in holiness. By having the limits of our lives exposed through the mutual telling of our stories, we discover that we are more together than we could ever be on our own.

So, distant though I may be from you, I'll do my best to find the time to tell you stories about people of faith that make my life possible and that I hope will contribute to your life too. Only such lives can free us from falsehood.

Your mother and father have asked me to write to you every year about a virtue that's im-

Your mother and father have asked me to write to you every year about a virtue that's important for living the Christian life. It's a welcome assignment that will force me to be articulate about matters I might otherwise leave unexamined.

portant for living the Christian life. It's a welcome assignment that will force me to be articulate about matters I might otherwise leave unexamined. But there's a danger in becoming so articulate that we might confuse thought and reflection with living well. Like me, your mother and father are people who have become what we call in the church "theologians." The church calls some out to think hard about the Christian faith, but I think you'll discover that the bearers of the virtues for sustaining the Christian faith aren't necessarily theologians. Instead, they're the people who, day in and day out, through small acts of tenderness and beauty, sustain the kind of life we call Christian. In short, Christians lead lives that would be unintelligible if God wasn't present to us through the life, death, and resurrection of Jesus Christ.

> *That you are made a Christian on this day will take you a lifetime to live into. It will be a life often challenged by the world that is aborning.*

That you are made a Christian on this day will take you a lifetime to live into. It will be a life often challenged by the world that is aborning. Being a Christian in such a world may well mean you won't be celebrated in the wider society in which you find yourself. We're living in what is often said to be an increasingly secular society, even though we have no idea what it means to call it secular. Still, at the very least, "secular" means you won't be able to assume that the practices of your society can be relied on for sustaining you as a Christian. I hope you'll find the lack of support to be a great good in that it will make you all the more joyful that you haven't had to choose who you will be but will know it has been given to you through the Holy Spirit at your baptism.

In the not-too-distant past, a man named Dietrich Bonhoeffer wrote a letter addressed to another boy on his baptism. Bonhoeffer had to write a letter not because he was a great distance away, but because he was in prison. He was there because he courageously opposed the virulent evil of Nazi Germany. Bonhoeffer's time was obviously one of great terror, but he wrote to his godson that he wished to live in no other time than the one that constituted his life—a time he recognized as a threat to his very being. Such a time, he observed, lies under both the wrath and the grace of God. In the letter he quoted Jeremiah 45, in which God says that what God has built will be torn down. Bonhoeffer concluded by saying, "If we can save our souls unscathed out of the wreckage of our material possessions, let us be satisfied with that."

Bonhoeffer noted that one of the reasons Christians failed to see the evil the Nazis represented was that pain had become a stranger to them. They sought unconsciously to be as free as possible from suffering and as a result lost their ability to live as Christians. Their desire to avoid suffering resulted in greater suffering—which was made all the more horrible because innocent people, the Jews, had to suffer because of Christians' unwillingness to do so. In fact, Bonhoeffer noted that Christians thought they could make their way in life guided only by reason and justice. When those ideals failed, they felt at the end of their tether.

It may seem strange to call attention to Bonhoeffer's reflections on the day of your baptism because it is often assumed that we live in a very different world than he did. It is often said that we live in a free society where people can do what they want to do and choose who they want to be. So we assume the totalitarian threat that Bonhoeffer so valiantly fought has been defeated. For this reason, your baptism doesn't appear to be a threat to your very existence.

But I urge you to be careful, because the soft worlds in which your mother and father and I live are in many ways more threatening than the world in which Bonhoeffer lived. They are so because the enemy is so hard to see, disguised as he is in clothes of sentimentality made possible by unimaginable wealth. You've been born into an extraordinarily wealthy society whose riches have often been acquired at the expense of others. The wealth of societies like America and England can be a great threat to the life you've been given through baptism in that it may tempt you and those around you to believe that you can live without suffering. But the baptism you undergo means that you've been made part of God's war against the powers which would possess our lives by tempting us to believe that Christians are not at war with war.

So I do not wish you will have an untroubled life, but I hope the troubles you confront will be those made necessary by your being made a member of the Body of Christ. Such troubles will mean you'll need many friends. And I hope you discover that nothing is more precious in the world than the gift of a friend. Friendship takes time, because we don't easily come

But in a world that believes time is in short supply, God has given us all the time we need to become friends with one another. And in becoming friends with each other, we learn to become friends with God. I hope you will come to count me as a friend.

to know one another. But in a world that believes time is in short supply, God has given us all the time we need to become friends with one another. And in becoming friends with each other, we learn to become friends with God. I hope you will come to count me as a friend.

For Laurence Bailey Wells on His Baptism

My profoundest wish for you is that as you grow, you grow confident in the faith. To be confident means you will never feel the need to protect God, because God doesn't need our protection. With the Psalmist you will learn to pray, at once despairing that your life isn't working out as you intended but remaining strong in your faith in God, who gives you the strength to be capable of despair. To be able to pray with such confidence is a great gift, and there's nothing more that I could wish for your life.

I pray, finally, for you to have a happy life. To be a Christian is to be invited to be part of God's creation, so that a Texas mockingbird and a loving dog (and cat) may fill us with joy. May you have a sense of humor made possible by such joy.

I look forward to the times when we might be together. May we laugh at and with one another.

Peace and love,

Stanley Hauerwas

Kindness

Dear Laurie,

I've been given the happy assignment to write to you every year on the anniversary of your baptism to reflect on a virtue. "Reflect on a virtue" may be too weak a description of my assignment. I am not only to reflect on but also to recommend a virtue I hope you discover you cannot live without. I use the grammar of "discover" because it would be a mistake for me to "urge you to develop" a virtue that may be missing in your life. For as I will indicate, my task is not so much to recommend but to help you name the virtues that already possess your life.

We have now met. My wife, Paula, and I came to see you, your mother and father, your sister, Jana, and Connie in Cambridge this year. It was wonderful to get to know you. You're an extremely contented young boy, accepting the world as you find it. That you should so accept the world is not surprising because you're surrounded by people and a dog who love one another and you. May you never take such love for granted.

Unfortunately, there are other things that surround us, and I have to report that this has been another year filled with war. Paula and I live in the United States of America. America is Rome, by which I mean we are a country that is so powerful that we can do what we want to do to other people and not fear the consequences. Americans are extremely frightened to live in a world in which we are so powerful, which is why we'll go to any length to make ourselves feel safe. So America has gone to war in Afghanistan and Iraq. I fear your generation will harvest the result.

This makes it all the more odd that I write to you on the first anniversary of your baptism to discuss the virtue of kindness. To be kind in a violent world is very dangerous, but fortunately you will discover you were destined to be kind. The Spirit of kindness stirred in the waters of your baptism, setting you on a difficult and rewarding journey. You are also surrounded by the kindness of your mother, your father, your sister, your friend, Jana, and, not least of all, your dog, Connie. Our gentle God created our kind to be kind by making it impossible for us to exist without caring for those both like and unlike us.

I'm not recommending that you try to be kind. As you grow up, you'll discover that you *are* kind. Oddly, we usually don't become virtuous by trying to be virtuous. The virtues ride on the back of forms of life we discover along the way. So you won't become kind because your mom or dad tells you to be "nice" to your newborn sister. It's not a bad thing for you to learn to be nice to her, but I suspect you'll find that kindness has already found its way into your life in the simple joy you receive from the pleasure Connie displays when you pet her. The virtues are, so to speak, pulled out of us by our loves. That's why it's natural for us to be kind—because we were created to be so.

> *The virtues are, so to speak, pulled out of us by our loves. That's why it's natural for us to be kind—because we were created to be so.*

In the book of Colossians (3:12–17), the Apostle Paul addresses us as "God's chosen ones" and tells us:

> clothe yourselves with compassion, kindness, humility, meekness, and patience. Bear with one another and, if anyone has a complaint against

another, forgive each other; just as the Lord has forgiven you, so you also must forgive. Above all, clothe yourselves with love, which binds everything together in perfect harmony. And let the peace of Christ rule in your hearts, to which indeed you were called in the one body. And be thankful. Let the word of Christ dwell in you richly; teach and admonish one another in all wisdom; and with gratitude in your hearts sing psalms, hymns, and spiritual songs to God. And whatever you do, in word or deed, do everything in the name of the Lord Jesus, giving thanks to God the Father through him.

You may well wonder why, on the first anniversary of your baptism, I've focused attention on the virtue of kindness. There are many virtues that are usually thought more important than kindness. Paul begins his list with compassion. He also tells us that "above all" we should clothe ourselves with love.

When the virtues have been discussed in the Christian tradition, love or charity has always been made the primary Christian virtue. Augustine, following Plato, suggested that all the virtues are forms of love. Aquinas, in a more Aristotelian vein, said that charity is the form of all the virtues. So why am I directing your attention to kindness when love is often considered to be the most important Christian virtue?

I could say I begin with kindness because it's the virtue relevant to your being a child. Young children usually aren't thought to have the capacity to be courageous, but it is often assumed you should be kind. Some also think there's a natural "cruelty" that comes with being a child. Children know they have needs, and they want their needs to be met immediately. For this reason, they sometimes don't recognize that others also have needs to be met.

I'm not recommending the virtue of kindness to you because I think it's peculiarly appropriate for children. I don't even believe that children lack the capacity to be courageous. But it's very important for the development of the virtues that we are rightly brought up. I believe our bodies, which is but another word for our passions, insure that the virtues we need for life beg to become actual in our habits. As you grow up, you'll discover most of the time that you don't have to try to be kind because you've become kind by having been raised in kindness.

I've begun with kindness because I believe kindness to be the very

> *I've begun with kindness because I believe kindness to be the very character of God.*

character of God. You were born and baptized in Norwich. An extraordinary Christian named Julian lived in Norwich during a time we now call the Middle Ages. She had a vision of God that is as wonderful as it is frightening. One of her famous claims is that "all shall be well, and all manner of things shall be well." Such a claim seems remarkable because the world in which she lived seemed anything but "well." So how did she know her claim was true? She says she knew because "God is kind in his very being." She knew of God's kindness because God became our "kind" in the life, death, and resurrection of Jesus Christ. Christians call this great mystery—the mystery of how Jesus was very God and very man—the Incarnation.

It is becasue our faith centers on the Incarnation that kindness is the very heart of the way we are called to live. We believe, even in a world as violent as the one in which we find ourselves, that we can risk being kind. We are called to be like God, but we are not called to be God. In fact, we believe we can be like God precisely because God is God and we are not. We are, like Connie and the rabbits in your backyard and the plants the rabbits eat, creatures. Another great Englishman, William Langland, in a poem called *Piers Plowman*, asked "what kind of thing is kind," answering that Kind

Is the creator of all kinds of beasts,
Father and former, the first of all things,
And that is the great God that had beginning
   never.
Lord of life and of light, of relief and of pain.

We are creatures created by kindness to be kind to all that is. It's often hard to distinguish kindness from compassion. Actually, it may be a mistake to think we need to distinguish between the two, even though Paul seems to do so in Colossians. If there's a difference between them, I suspect it's no more than that kindness names a relation to our fellow creatures whether they're suffering or not. Compassion suggests our need to be with, to suffer with, our fellow creatures in the bad times as well as the good times.

To be kind is to learn how to be a creature with other creatures without regret. To be kind is to learn how to receive kindness from others without protection. To be kind is to be drawn into God's good creation without fear. To be kind is to be

> *To be kind is to learn how to be a creature with other creatures without regret. To be kind is to learn how to receive kindness from others without protection.*

disposed to trust the gifts of others that quite literally make life possible. To be kind is to know when not to speak because nothing can be said that is not false. To be kind is the willingness to be present when nothing can be said or done to make things better.

One of the ways we try to understand the nature of a virtue is by contrast with its opposite. The opposite of a virtue is called a vice. Often there are several vices that can be contrasted to a virtue, but the contrary vice of kindness is singular and clear. It is called cruelty. I suggested above that children are often thought to be "naturally" cruel because they haven't learned to regard the needs of others. But to so attribute cruelty to children is usually a mistake. Children may sometimes act cruelly, but children are seldom cruel.

I suspect that in general we don't like to think that anyone is cruel "on purpose," but unfortunately some people have developed a steady disregard for others that is rightly called cruelty. And because we're extremely subtle creatures, we can actually disguise our cruelty as a kind of regard for the well-being of others. Once the habits of cruelty are learned, we can't change them by simply trying to will our way free of them. Instead, we must be offered a new way of life that can come in small steps—steps as simple as asking forgiveness from one to whom we have been cruel.

I suspect you'll find that you're seldom tempted to be cruel. The greatest threat to our being virtuous usually comes not from vice but from dispositions that are similar to virtue. The great enemy of kindness, for example, is sentimentality. Sentimentality is the greater enemy of the life of virtue just to the extent that sentimentality names the assumption that we can be kind without being truthful. Sentimentality mocks kindness by confusing the public display of concern with genuine tenderness. Sentimentality hides the ugly truth that our gestures of recognition are actually expressions of our self-centeredness.

You won't always be able to tell if you're being kind or sentimental. Most often we're only able to come to some understanding of our habitual dispositions and actions retrospectively. To have the appropriate self-knowledge that kindness requires means you will need good friends. Through such friendships you will be able to see who you are becoming, who you are, and to whom you belong. You belong to God, to God's people, the Church, and all those whose kindness makes it possible for you to be kind.

You will have noticed that kindness, like all the other virtues, cannot stand alone. For kindness to be rescued from sentimentality requires the vir-

> *You will have noticed that kindness, like all the other virtues, cannot stand alone. For kindness to be rescued from sentimentality requires the virtue of honesty.*

tue of honesty. Over the years we'll explore how the virtues are individually named as well as how they interrelate. We will also see how each virtue will bear the mark of the challenges and opportunities peculiar to your life. For example, not everyone will have Connie to love and care for. But we believe that God gives each of us all we need to find our way to kindness. We believe that God gave his Son that we might be freed from the temptation to treat others cruelly in the name of a good cause. Now, take joy in the life you have been given, because joy makes possible the way of kindness.

In Christ,

Stanley

Truthfulness

Dear Laurie,

Paula and I visited your home at the end of April, so we have some idea of what it means to be Laurie. It's a joy to see you grow, and not only you, but also your sister, Stephanie, whom we also met. You and Stephanie are a joy to be with because you both so enjoy life. You love balls. In particular, you like to kick balls, which is good because football (what you English call football) is a major sport (in England). I suppose it's a bit of a disadvantage that one of your godfathers is an American. I'll never understand the sports you will no doubt come to love.

In my last letter to you, I wrote about the dark times in which we find ourselves. I wish I could report that the world is getting better, but I'm afraid that matters are even worse. The war America and

England have waged in Iraq, a war that some who planned it called "optional," hasn't gone well. Americans and the English "won" the war only to discover that "winning" means we must now impose on an Arab nation a government they don't want. In short, the situation is a mess. This makes it all the more important for you to enjoy the wonder that is your life.

One of the wonders in your life is that you're beginning to talk. Paula and I are sure we heard you say "da-da," and by the time you get this letter, your vocabulary will have been enriched. Before you know it, you'll be talking in sentences. The world is constituted by words in a way that makes it difficult to distinguish between us and the world. One of the wonders of our lives is that we don't have to create the world because God has made it possible for us to enjoy—and would have us share his delight in—what he has created. Creation is gift. Our task is to learn to receive. Language is one of the gifts, perhaps one of the most precious gifts, that help us receive God's grace and the gifts of God's good creation.

We have been created with tongues. Almost all of God's creatures have tongues, but our tongues are special. They allow us to make wonderful sounds of infinite variety. The flexibility of our tongues also makes it possible for us to develop languages so that we might communicate with one another. But we need to be cautious not to turn this gift into a prideful claim that makes us different from the rest of God's creation, because other animals also develop languages and can communicate. Still, humans do seem to have been given a special gift of language that makes possible a rich communal life.

If we are to be communal, if we are to be able to communicate, we must speak truthfully to one another. That's the virtue I want to commend to you on the second anniversary of your baptism. Interestingly, truthfulness is seldom named as a primary virtue in Christian theological reflection. We're usually told not to lie, but avoiding lying doesn't necessarily make us truthful. Truthfulness may be one of those virtues so central to our lives that it's invisible. But we must be careful not to let this "invisibility" hide from us the centrality of truth for being able to live peaceably with one another.

In the book of Ephesians, the Apostle Paul urges that we speak the "truth in love" to one another in order that we might "grow up in every way into him who is the head, into Christ, from whom the whole body, joined and knit together by every ligament with which it is equipped, as each part is working properly, promotes the body's growth in building itself up in love" (Eph. 4:15–16). Paul notes further that we—that is, those of us claimed by Christ—are freed from greediness and impurity because we've been taught the truth in Christ. So taught, we are to "[put] away falsehood" so we can "speak the truth to our neighbors, for we are members of one another" (Eph. 4:25). And in the book of Revelation we are told that those who practice falsehood will often find themselves grouped with murderers and idolaters (Rev. 22:15).

These passages from Scripture help us see why and how truthfulness is so important for our ability to live at peace with one another. I suspect some become murderers because they're so determined to make the lies that have constituted their lives true. In other words, the perversions that so often grip our lives do so not because we're bad people, but because we desire to be good, to tell the truth. But the desire to speak truthfully, a desire meant to lead us to God, corrupts our lives when we fail to live the truth we've been taught Christ is. This distance between how we live and what we know to be true is painful and tempts us to change the truth rather than change our lives.

We were created to communicate, to speak truthfully to one another, so that we might be members of one another. To be members of one another means we must learn to trust one another. Trust, like truthfulness, is a gift that is essential to our lives if we are to live with one another. When the trust that truth makes possible is lost, our lives cannot help but be captured by forms of violence—violence often disguised as order and, for that reason, not recognized for the lie that is at its heart.

That's why any peace that isn't truthful is cursed. We should be grateful that the peace constituted by truthfulness is at once hard work and entertaining. In fact, if peace weren't hard work, it wouldn't be entertaining. Peace rides on the back of truthful speech, requiring that we not confuse the absence of violence with peace. That's why truthfulness is deeper than the lie. The lie is always parasitic on truth.

A word often used to describe the virtue of truthfulness is honesty. Honesty no doubt gestures toward truthfulness, but honesty usually denotes straightforward forms of behavior. You hear people say, "He did the honest thing." Honesty is necessary for our ability to be truthful, but honesty doesn't capture the full reality of being truthful. To cheat is to fail to be honest, and lying can be thought to be a form of cheating. But to speak truthfully means we sometimes must say what must be said even when we don't necessarily "owe" the truth to the one to whom we speak. Still, this isn't an invitation for cruelty.

As you know, I am a Texan. Texans pride ourselves on being "straight shooters." We think we ought to tell it "the way it is." As a result, we often confuse candor and truthfulness. The truth will often hurt, but that doesn't mean hurting someone is an indication of having told the truth. To be truthful doesn't mean that we must say what needs to be said bluntly. Just the opposite is often the case. We must say what needs to be said in such a manner that it can be received. Regrettably, this requirement can also be used to excuse the failure to tell the truth.

> *To be truthful doesn't mean that we must say what needs to be said bluntly. Just the opposite is often the case. We must say what needs to be said in such a manner that it can be received.*

This is but a reminder that being truthful is a skill that requires constant practice and vigilance. What was said at one time and place may have been truthful, but at another time and place may not be truthful. Dietrich Bonhoeffer (remember my meditation on your baptism?), in a wonderful essay called "What Is Meant by 'Telling the Truth'?," observes that telling the truth isn't simply a matter of character; it's also a matter of appreciating "real situations." By this Bonhoeffer means that we must respond to what's really going on if we're to understand how we should speak as Christians. Bonhoeffer then suggests that "telling the truth is something which must be learnt," and the learning is never finished because it's part of our ongoing life with God.

On this basis, Bonhoeffer argues that the usual definition of a lie as the conscious discrepancy between thought and speech is inadequate. Note that he doesn't say such a view is wrong, just inadequate. The problem is that no formal account of lying does justice to the complex art of truthfulness. That art turns out to be one that acknowledges the God who has evidenced himself in Christ to the world. Bonhoeffer quotes 1 John 2:22 and then elaborates:

> "Who is a liar but he that denieth that Jesus is the Christ." The lie is a contradiction of the word of God, which God has spoken in Christ, and upon which creation is founded. Consequently the lie is the denial, the negation and the conscious and deliberate destruction of the reality which is created by God and which consists in God, no matter whether this purpose is achieved by speech or by silence. The assigned purpose of our silence is to signify the limit which is imposed upon our words by the real as it exists in God.

I know this is deep stuff, but it's important because Bonhoeffer is getting at something you'll want to hold on to for the future. You'll notice that in commending truthfulness, following Bonhoeffer, I've begun to speak of the lie. With every gift and every virtue comes a dark side. The dark side of truthfulness is lying. No doubt the lie can involve our intentional attempt to mislead someone, but it is often difficult to distinguish between the lie and the truth, even for one who wants to speak the truth, for lies inhabit our speech. We speak them as truth because everyone speaks them as truth.

So this is a reminder that if we are to speak truthfully, we need the help of the church to expose the lies that would speak through us.

But if we are created to be truthful, to worship God faithfully, why would we ever lie? The reasons for our penchant to lie make a very long list. Pride and power are names for aspects of our lives that often tempt us to lie. Notice, for example, how you acquired and lost power as you learned to speak. As long as you pointed to what you wanted, you had your mom and dad under your control. They had to guess what you wanted or what would satisfy you. But when you learned to name things, you lost power, because now you could be reasoned with. By learning to speak, you have begun the unending process through which we unlearn our self-fascination, because speech entails a responsibility to others.

Once a child is able to verbally communicate, it becomes his duty to try to communicate well. This is a loss, to be sure, but also a wonderful gain because the power of communication makes us more than we ever could have imagined.

We often lie because as prideful beings we don't want our limits exposed. We fear our foolishness will be laid bare. We create false worlds that we then inhabit, making it impossible to distinguish the real from the false. We're also very good at making our lies seem true. That's why the exposure of our lies is often so dramatic. We quite literally must be forced from our illusions by a more determinative reality. Some people are so good at living lies (and the lies that constitute our lives often take the dreaded form of the half-truth), they end up living out a life that is not their own. Self-deception, which is a deeper reality than "lying to ourselves," is a fate worse than death. In fact, self-deception is a kind of death because it causes us to lose our ability to be what God has called us to be: creatures who take delight in the world we have not created.

To speak the truth means we must be what we seem to be.

One of the ways this was once put is that we should be people of character. Above I called your attention to Bonhoeffer's observation that telling the truth isn't simply a matter of character. That's true, but without character we can't help but lose our way amid the lies that tempt us to live as if God doesn't exist. If we are to live truthfully, we must be able to confess our sins and, so confessing, have our sins forgiven.

As you grow up, I suspect you'll discover that it's easier to forgive than it is to be forgiven. Being forgiven, however, is what it means to be Christian. Through forgiveness we are freed from our vain attempts to be our own creators, and we discover the truth about ourselves.

I hope my focus on the virtue of truthfulness doesn't lead you to despair. It seems so hard to be truthful and to speak truthfully. But even though it can be hard, most of the time we can speak the truth because to so speak makes us joyful.

God has given us a wonderful exercise for training in truthfulness. That exercise is called prayer. To learn to pray is to have our bodies formed by the truth and love that move the sun and the stars.

God has given us a wonderful exercise for training in truthfulness. That exercise is called prayer. To learn to pray is to have our bodies formed by the truth and love that move the sun and the stars. I recommend that you pray the great prayers of the church that have been honed by the saints through the centuries so that we say no more and no less than needs to be said to God. Such prayers are the benchmark of truthful speech by which we learn to praise and thank God for the wonder that is our life.

Peace and love,

Stanley

P.S. I think it's time for an addendum to these letters. Paula asked me if I'm writing these to be published, and the answer is partly yes. As you grow up, you'll discover I've written a great deal that is published. That I have done so is both a blessing and a curse. It's a blessing because what I've written has brought people into my life who have claimed me as a friend—your parents being prime examples. It's a curse because I've become "famous," at least as famous as a theologian can be in our world. My way of putting that fame is to note that I never meant to become Stanley Hauerwas, but I have to acknowledge that I've become something called "Stanley Hauerwas" for both the good and the ill that come from it. So I'm quite aware that these letters will be read by people other than you who will read them in the hope of better understanding Stanley Hauerwas.

That said, I do try to remember I'm writing them to you. Some people may object that cannot be the case because you won't be able to "get" these letters until you're much older.

Let me explain. I don't write in such a way that you'll be able to read these letters now or even have them read to you while you're a child. I just don't know how to write to someone very young. I wish I did, but I don't possess the talent or the art for that high calling. So I write in the hope that when you're older, you'll read these letters and may discover a sentence here or there that helps you name the virtues that constitute your life.

So I write in the hope that when you're older, you'll read these letters and may discover a sentence here or there that helps you name the virtues that constitute your life.

Friendship

≈ *Third Anniversary: October 27, 2005* ≈

Dear Laurie,

Soon you'll be living in America. How extraordinary! Your father and mother have accepted positions at Duke University. Your father will be Dean of the Chapel at Duke, and your mother will be on the faculty at the Divinity School. I couldn't be happier with the prospect of your family being in Durham, North Carolina, and at Duke, since Paula and I also work there. This means we'll really get to know one another. Your father has already said that now I'm the godparent in residence. A thought, I must say, that takes me back a bit, because I've never been sure how to be a godparent.

I rather like writing these long-distance letters because I'm afraid my own life is a good deal less virtuous than the virtues I recommend. Still, Paula and I are delighted, joyful, and thrilled that y'all (remember, we're from the South) will be here. But we're also apprehensive. The problem is not, as many conservative Americans claim, that the country you are moving to, the United States, is a decadent culture. England, I suspect, certainly deserves that description more than America. Decadence, after all, requires a fairly high cultural achievement. The American problem of decadence is a shallowness captured by the American concern that "we just all get along." There is a nastiness to the Brits that can be quite attractive when contrasted to the American demand to be nice at all times.

I don't worry about your being corrupted by American culture because you're the son of Sam and Jo. Not only will they never let you forget that you're really English, but they will insure that your life will be surrounded by beauty, goodness, and truth. This is but another way to say that they will make sure that you worship God (and it is my duty to see that they do this). No doubt you'll often be in Duke Chapel, which is a beautiful building where the music during services is glorious, but Paula and I hope you'll also be able to worship with us at the Church of the Holy Family. We're a modest place compared to Duke Chapel, but modesty can often be quite beautiful too.

So I'm not so much worried about the effects of American culture on you. But I am worried that if you're here for some time, you may find it very hard to resist the attraction of American power. America is an extremely seductive reality. You'll hear over and over again, "America is the most powerful country in the world." And you'll be inclined to believe this because American economic and military might is truly overwhelming. To be part of the most powerful country in the world cannot help but seize the imagination. Even when you're critical of the use of American power, it's still hard to learn to resist identifying with such a powerful country. One can't help but be tempted to believe that the problem is not having so much power but the uses to which that power is put. You may find it almost impossible to resist the thought that your task is to make the power of America serve the good.

I'm often identified as a radical critic of American ambitions, and I fear the "radical" posture is more American than Christian. It's hard to keep your head, to stay calm, when the world around you seems to be going mad. In America, this has been particularly true after September 11, 2001. The most powerful country in the world runs on fear. It does so because most Americans live as if we don't have to die. And we're ready to put the rest of the world at risk if that's what it takes to preserve our denial of death.

But I am an American, and I love this country. More important, by critiquing it, I don't want to avoid being an American. I love the beauty and variety of the American landscape, I love the diversity of her people, I love the spirit and energy of Americans, and I love our food, which is usually not "ours" but Italian, Mexican, or Asian. I also love the American work ethic. America is constituted by great goods, but goods too often perverted by American pride and pretension.

You will discover things (or at least I hope you will) about the roots and history of the United States that are devastating—that Americans in the past slaughtered Native Americans, and that we were a slave-holding nation. These are stubborn "facts" that remain largely unacknowledged in American public discourse. Americans, like all people, find it difficult to acknowledge wrongs that are so wrong there is nothing they can do to make them right. The sad result is that America remains a country in denial. Denial results in a selective loss of memory that is then replaced by the pursuit of wealth and happiness. The future, not the past, is the focus of American life. We're convinced that if all people had our education, political system, and money, they would want to be just like us. That presumption makes us a very dangerous people.

It also makes America a very dangerous place for Christians. The temptation is to confuse American "ideals" with Christian practice. Christians in America often seem to think that Jesus came to establish democratic societies and governments. They do so because they believe the church is "free" in America. These are very dangerous assumptions for Christians to make because too often they lead to the further assumption that if Americans need to kill someone to insure democracy, they should do so. As a result, Christian loyalty to America threatens the unity of the church.

This finally brings me to the virtue I want to recommend on the third anniversary of your baptism. I've gone on so long that you may have begun to wonder if I had forgotten my task in these letters. I'm going to recommend a virtue, but your coming to America has made a difference in how I have to think about this assignment. If you rightly understand the virtues, you realize that they're meant not to protect us but rather to help us negotiate the dangers of the world in which we find ourselves. This is why I think as you grow up, at least for a while in America, you will find nothing quite so important as the virtue of friendship.

Friendship is a strange virtue, because it isn't clear it *is* a virtue. Aristotle begins Book Eight of *The Nicomachean Ethics* observing that friendship is "a virtue, or involves a virtue." He's unsure if friendship is a virtue because he's unsure what the habit of friendship habituates. After all, friendship is a relationship, but how can a habit qualify as a relationship? That's why Aristotle suggests that friendship "involves a virtue," but still seems to think that virtue should be called friendship. In fact, he even says in the next sentence that friendship is the virtue "most necessary for life." He does so, I think, because he rightly believes that all the virtues are tested by their ability to sustain good friendships.

This is extremely important because Americans are very friendly, but we aren't very good at being friends. Friendship, at least friendship that is a virtue, turns out to be very demanding. Aristotle, for example, suggests that most friendships are friendships of use or pleasure. These relationships come to an end when friends no longer have need of one another or no longer enjoy the same pleasures. And I'm afraid that Americans assume that there is no alternative to such friendships.

But Aristotle thought there could be a form of friendship that was lasting. He believed that a friendship would last if the friends shared a common love of virtue. Accordingly, Aristotle thought we were incapable of being a friend if we were not our own best friend. Being our own best friend may sound "egoistic," but I think Aristotle is on to something. But I also think that what it might mean to be our own best friend can be quite perverse if we lack the resources given to us in the gospel. For if I am able to befriend myself, I must first be able to be forgiven by another.

That's a remark that I hope illumines why, as attractive as Aristotle's understanding of virtuous friendship may be, it is also limited. Aristotle, for example, thought it unlikely that you and I might become friends because he didn't think the young were capable of becoming virtuous. He also thought friendship between old people (and I am an old person) and young people was impossible because the difference in ages just made them too dissimilar. He would have thought that you and I don't have enough in common to be friends. We may well find these judgments severe, but we must also acknowledge that whether we like it or not, what Aristotle has to say about the difficulty of true friendship is unfortunately often the case—unless we are Christians.

In the Gospel of John, Jesus calls his disciples his friends, saying, "You are my friends if you do what I command you. I do not call you servants any longer, because the servant does not know what the master is doing; but I have called you friends, because I have made known to you everything that I have heard from my Father. You did not choose me but I chose you. And I appointed you to go and bear fruit, fruit that will last, so that the Father will give you whatever you ask him in my name. I am giving you these commands so that you may love one another" (15:14–17). Jesus, in a manner that Aristotle wouldn't have understood, says he can make us friends with himself and even with one another. He can do so because he is the Son of God, the Second Person of the Trinity, claiming us by a love that moves the sun and the stars. If Jesus can make us his friends, then in spite of the difference in our ages—or because of that difference—you and I may become friends.

How extraordinary that God would want to make us friends! What could that possibly mean? I don't pretend to be able to give a satisfactory answer to that question, but I think surely it involves learning to pray. For if Aristotle is right to say that friendship involves a virtue, prayer is surely the kind of habituation that makes friendship possible. To learn to pray means our lives must be made vulnerable to God. It requires time and patience to wait on the Lord, and surely the same time and patience are what make friendship possible. We live in a world that seems to think these goods are in short supply. Yet, as Christians, we believe that God has given us all the time and patience necessary to be friends to one another and with God. The Irish Catholic priest Enda McDonagh, a friend of mine, once told me that prayer is the way we make God loose in the world—a frightening thought, given the wild presence the Holy Spirit is. What could it mean to "loose God" into the world other than our showing the world how God has overcome our impatience by teaching us to befriend one another—and even our enemies?

To be a friend requires, consequently, the readiness to be surprised, because we can never anticipate how God may show up. Who, after all, could have anticipated God showing up as Jesus? In the Gospel of Matthew, Jesus tells "the righteous" that they failed to welcome him, for "I was hungry and you gave me no food, I was thirsty and you gave me nothing to drink, I was a stranger and you did not welcome me, naked and you did not give me clothing, sick and in prison and you did not visit me." "The righteous" object that they didn't see him in such a condition, but Jesus responds, "Truly I tell you, just as you did not do it to one of the least of these, you did not do it to me" (Matt. 25:42–46).

Christians believe we have all the time in the world for strangers to become friends. (Some of those strangers may be those creatures we call animals, like Connie. Never forget that you also are an animal, and that befriending Connie has taught you something important about how a stranger may become a friend.) Hospitality is surely the virtue—a virtue unknown to Aristotle—that makes it possible for Christians to hope that strangers will become our friends: Christians believe that we have friends we didn't know we had. For example, how could I ever have anticipated that an Englishman named Sam Wells would claim me as a friend? Our biographies don't suggest we would have "naturally" been friends. For one thing, your father is a good deal more "cultured" than I could ever pretend to be. Remember, I am a Texan. But friends we are. And I believe we're friends because we discovered that God had led us to share common judgments. "Judgments" is a name for commitments made through time that constitute a history that becomes a way of life. I have sometimes called this "character."

Because your father claimed me as a friend, we have discovered that our friendship is enriched by our coming to love one another through those we love and who love us. I would not be me without Paula, and Sam would not be Sam without Jo. Friendship is tricky, but friendships between couples are particularly tricky. It's important that everyone (as we say in the South) is "all growed up." So Paula and I are particularly grateful that we're friends with your parents, because without that friendship our lives would be less rich.

Of course, the problem with friendships is that they can and usually do change our lives. That your father claimed me as a friend means that you will now live in America. I need to be clear about this. It's not my fault that your parents got their positions at Duke. This was their doing and the doing of those at Duke who rightly saw that they had gifts that Duke needed. But it's probably true that your father's claiming me as a friend some years ago began the process that means you will now be living in America. All life is contingency, and contingency is the very "stuff" that makes friendship possible. For what is friendship but the discovery that I don't want to tell my story—can't tell my story—without your story? So you can see why I feel some responsibility for your being in America, and why I

> *All life is contingency, and contingency is the very "stuff" that makes friendship possible. For what is friendship but the discovery that I don't want to tell my story—can't tell my story—without your story?*

hope your becoming American (and I suspect there's no way you'll avoid absorbing America) will always be tested through the friends that claim you in the name of Christ.

The Church names friendships across time and space, made possible through the work of the Holy Spirit. You have been baptized by that Spirit, which means you'll discover that your life is constituted by a network of friendship it will take a lifetime to discover. You may well wonder if such a network of friendship is sufficient to counter the power of America. I can tell you that there will be times when you will rightly wonder if you're on the losing side. But don't despair. Friends are but another name for hope, and you have many friends. Those friends—friends in Uganda, friends in Ethiopia, friends in Ireland, friends in Australia, friends in America, friends in England, Catholic friends, Jewish friends, friends in positions of power, friends who are mentally handicapped, friends who are rich, friends who are poor—will help you do the good work in virtue, as virtue.

Of course, I certainly hope I will be counted among your friends. But just as important, I hope you'll learn to rejoice in the friends you discover you didn't know you had through our friendship. For Christians, friendship is not a zero-sum game. We believe our friendships make friendships with others possible. So welcome to America, for even here you will be befriended by God, making it possible for you to be in friendship with God's people in all manner of times and in all manner of places.

> *For Christians, friendship is not a zero-sum game. We believe our friendships make friendships with others possible.*

In friendship,

Stan

Patience

Dear Laurie,

By now you've lived in Durham, North Carolina, for a year, and we've gotten to know one another a bit. I thoroughly enjoy watching you play and interact with your family, friends, and dog. (But your family should get you a cat too.) You have the energy with which the young are blessed. I don't try to keep up with you, and I hope that's a sign of some wisdom. I know it would be a mistake for me to try to be for you what I'm not—young. But I don't want to pretend I know what it means to be "grown up," even though I'll be sixty-six this summer. I keep thinking I should know what it means, but I find I'm as clueless about negotiating life at this age as I was when I was younger.

Because we now live in the same city, I know I need to write more personal letters to you. You're going to grow up here, so there's no way either of us can avoid getting to know each other. When you lived in England, I found I could write to you more easily because I could assume that you would know me primarily through these letters. But now you're really going to get to know me. I confess that frightens me a bit, because, as I mentioned before, you will surely discover that the virtues I recommend I don't necessarily exhibit in my life. So for me to write to you every year recommending a virtue can't help but feel a bit pretentious. Just try to remember that I am, in good faith, doing what your parents asked me to do.

On the fourth anniversary of your baptism, I want to recommend to you the virtue of patience, which I take to be one of the central virtues for Christians. Patience didn't seem all that important to the Greeks or Romans. In fact, it's not even clear that they had a name for patience, though they may have recognized something like the importance of patience as an aspect of courage or endurance. But it's very important that the virtues have names, because the names of virtues depend on the basic stories a community tells about itself. And the virtues make the community's stories necessary. As I will suggest below, I think it's no accident that patience was discovered by Christians.

But before I say more about patience, I need to be as candid with you as I can. No virtue is more important to me than the virtue of patience. Yet I'm one of the most impatient people you'll ever meet. I'm always feeling impatient, wanting to get things done. I'm a person with great energy, which leads me to think it's always better to do something than to do nothing. I felt this way even when I was young. When my parents gave me small jobs, what we called "chores," I wanted to get the first one done quickly in order to get on to the next one, which I would also do quickly.

But now that I'm older, I think my impatience has something to do with the fact that I tend to be an angry person. I don't want to scare you by calling attention to my anger, because I can also be quite gentle. But it's true that I don't just get angry at this or that, but that I *am* angry. I'm not sure where my anger comes from, but it seems always to have fueled everything I do. I like to think my anger is partly due to my being such a passionate person, someone born with a passion to make a difference. As a result, I assault the world because I simply can't refrain from trying to do that. Many, quite understandably, find me tiresome to be around.

In general, anger has a bad name, and no doubt there are times when I'm inappropriately angry. But if I'm right that my impatience is related to my anger, it does offer a clue to the virtues about which I have only hinted in my previous letters. Many of the virtues involve the habituation of the passions. The virtues do not so much "control" the passions as the virtues form the passions so that our desires become the source of what makes us capable of goodness. For that reason, anger isn't necessarily a "bad thing" to have. In fact, we are often appropriately angry, but our anger needs to be formed by the habit of patience so that it is rightly directed.

Many of the virtues involve the habituation of the passions. The virtues do not so much "control" the passions as the virtues form the passions so that our desires become the source of what makes us capable of goodness.

Honestly, I was fortunate to be formed by habits that should have made me more patient than I am. I was brought up to be a bricklayer. To learn to lay bricks—at least, to learn to lay bricks well—takes time. But to learn to do this requires that you start by building other skills. First you must learn how to labor for bricklayers—how to chop mud, pitch brick, build scaffold, joint, and innumerable other tasks. Learning to labor takes infinite patience because your task is to do whatever the bricklayers ask, and often what they ask is unreasonable. But I was a very good laborer.

I was first taken to "the job" when I was seven years old, and by the time I was ten I could do the work of a man. But my father didn't teach me to lay brick until I was sixteen. I know I often frustrated my poor father, a master craftsman, because at first I thought it more important to lay as many bricks a day as I could, which meant that sometimes I didn't pay close attention to *how* I laid the bricks. Eventually I became a pretty good bricklayer, though I would never be able to lay brick as beautifully as my father could.

Learning to lay brick is just one way to learn to be patient. You'll discover patience through learning to read, playing games, and countless other activities. Patience is the habit of time because time is the incarnation of habit. Habits may become second nature to us, but we need to remember how fundamental they are for determining who we are.

Patience is the habit of time because time is the incarnation of habit. Habits may become second nature to us, but we need to remember how fundamental they are for determining who we are.

Our bodies beg to be formed by habits, so it's very important that we are formed well early on. I'm sure, for example, that the habits I learned by laying brick continue to shape my work as a teacher and theologian. I work hard and I hope well, but I also continue to work too much in a hurry. I want to change the world, and I rush because I arrogantly think that "my work" is important for the changes I desire to see.

Yet, as I've mentioned, impatient though I may be, I'm sure no virtue is more important for learning to be a Christian than patience. As you might expect, I didn't readily come to understand the significance of patience as a central virtue for being Christian. In the face of the injustices that grip our lives, I thought patience was at best a counsel of despair. But once I finally began to understand why, as followers of Christ, we must learn to live nonviolently, I couldn't avoid the recognition that patience is the virtue necessary to sustain a people who have disavowed violence as a means to settle disputes.

My way of putting the matter goes like this. Christians aren't called to live nonviolently in a world of war because we believe our nonviolence is a strategy to rid the world of war. Instead, as faithful followers of Christ in a world of war, we can't imagine being anything other than nonviolent. Christian nonviolence may even make the world more violent because the world doesn't want the appearance of order, what it will sometimes call "peace," exposed for what it is. In other words, the world often justifies violence as a way of maintaining order. But this means that the appearance of order is often a mask for violence. So if nonviolence is a truthful alternative to the world's violence, you can expect the world to react violently to this alternative. Such a stance doesn't mean that Christians don't want to make war unlikely—even see it abolished—but we can be under no illusion that war and violence will be easily overthrown.

Many, including many Christians, regard such a stance as irresponsible. To be committed to nonviolence seems to make us complicit with evil. Yet as many have argued, the Christian stance of nonviolence is at the heart of the gospel. For we believe that in the crucifixion of Jesus, God refused to defeat our rebellion by crushing us. Instead, the Father's love of the Son overwhelmed our violence by refusing to end our violence violently. The word for God's forbearance, a forbearance exemplified in the cross of Christ, is patience. And as God is, so we are to be. In Revelation 13:9–10, we are told this:

> Let anyone who has an ear listen:
>   If you are to be taken captive,

into captivity you go;
if you kill with the sword,
 with the sword you must be killed.
Here is a call for the endurance and faith of the
 saints.

On the first anniversary of your baptism I called your attention to Colossians 3:12–17, in which Paul says, "Clothe yourselves with compassion, kindness, humility, meekness, and patience. Bear with one another and, if anyone has a complaint against another, forgive each other; just as the Lord has forgiven you, so you also must forgive. Above all, clothe yourselves with love, which binds everything together in perfect harmony." That patience comes at the end of the list of the virtues is not accidental. For without patience, love becomes sentimentality, which is not, like love, capable of binding all the virtues in harmony. Love entails patience because it describes how our lives are bound to others and to God. Sentimentality is self-serving and describes only our feelings about such-and-such. For example, some people claim their support of aborting children with Down syndrome is "compassion."

That Paul ends his list of virtues with patience is also telling because he's advising the Colossians about how to conduct themselves in relation to one another. My point here is that you will be brought up in the church, and you will be frustrated by the people who make up the church. You may even become as angry as I am with other Christians. But you must also be patient, which means you must be as ready to forgive as to be forgiven. The community necessary to be the church takes time—time determined by patience. You'll be frustrated by the time it takes for people to be who God would have us be, but remember that God has given us all the time in the world so that we might be patient with one another—even Stephanie.

By now you may be wondering if I've lost my hold on reality. You're just four years old. Patience, at least the kind of patience I've tried to suggest is the very heart of God, seems like a pretty heavy burden to put on a child. But if you think about it, it's also a pretty heavy burden to put on someone as impatient as I am. Which is just a way of reminding us both that the virtues aren't recommendations for individual achievement. The truth is that we can be patient only through being made patient through the patient love of others. That is the love I see surrounding you, making it possible for you to begin to acquire patience.

I say this because, as I have suggested with the other virtues, patience isn't "foreign" to our nature.

We were created to be patient because, as I noted earlier, we are bodily creatures. As you grow older, you'll notice that you'll want to do many things you see older children and adults doing. And you'll be frustrated because often you won't be able to do what they do so effortlessly. This kind of competence will require you to practice so that you will acquire the skills, the habits, that are necessary to do what they do. Practice is just another name for patience.

One of the practices of patience I hope you'll want to develop is called baseball. Baseball is America's greatest gift to civilization. It is a slow game of failure. If you win half the time, that's considered very good. Not only that, but a game takes nine innings, and the season is very long. During a game it often seems that little is happening. Of course, this is true only for those who don't understand the game. It takes extended training in patience to be a baseball fan because you must acquire the habits that allow you to see how compelling and beautiful this game of

One of the practices of patience I hope you'll want to develop is called baseball. Baseball is America's greatest gift to civilization. It is a slow game of failure. If you win half the time, that's considered very good.

peace is. But I hope that you'll want to do more than learn to watch baseball. I hope you'll want to *play* baseball. Learning to catch and hit is very hard, but having learned to do both will make you happy.

That baseball is the great American sport indicates that there is hope even for America. Americans pride themselves on speed, but speed is often just another name for violence. And as I suggested in some of my earlier letters to you, America is a very violent country. That we are so has everything to do with our impatience. But we do have baseball as an alternative to war. In one of my favorite novels, *The Brothers K*, David James Duncan agrees with me:

> I cherish a theory I once heard propounded by G. Q. Durham that professional baseball is inherently antiwar. The most overlooked cause of war, his theory runs, is that it is so damned interesting. It takes hard effort, skill, love and a little luck to make times of peace consistently interesting. About all it takes to make war interesting is a life. The appeal of trying to kill others without being killed yourself is that it brings suspense, terror, honor, disgrace, rage, tragedy, treachery and occasionally even heroism within range of guys who, in times of peace, might lead lives of un-mitigated blandness. But baseball is one activity

that is able to generate suspense and excitement on a national scale, just like war. And baseball can only be played in peace. Hence G. Q.'s thesis that pro ballplayers—little as some of them want to hear it—are basically a bunch of unusually well-co-ordinated guys working hard and artfully to prevent wars, by making peace more interesting.

Your father may well try to convince you that some game called cricket is actually more a game of peace than baseball, but you'll discover that baseball is far more compelling. At the very least, I promise to take you to ball games in order for you to learn from baseball the habits of peace. Which is but a reminder that the patience of nonviolence is not an ideal, but rather lies at the heart of the practices and habits that sustain our everyday life. As I've suggested, our very bodies were given to us so that we might learn to be patient.

I'm acutely aware that our bodies were given us to teach us patience because I am, as I mentioned at the beginning of this letter, growing old. I simply can't do what I once did, though I'm still trying to play baseball—at least I'm still trying to play church softball. In doing so, I'm having to learn how to be patient with myself, which isn't easy. So, as we grow older together, I hope you'll help me learn to be patient. I expect that you will because I'll have to learn how to be with you, and I'm not used to being with children. But I know that children are God's gift to us to slow us down. And I look forward to our learning how to be patient with one another.

Impatiently yours,

Stan

Hope

Dear Laurie,

I'm sixty-seven, but you are just five years old. Dare I write to you about death? Death is no longer a theoretical possibility for me. But for you, death is not, so to speak, in the game. And that's the way it should be. Still, I'm writing to commend to you the virtue of hope—and hope means that the subject of death cannot be avoided.

I must have been close to your age the first time I confronted death. My family went to a classic Methodist church in Pleasant Mound, Texas. "Classic" means it was a white frame building crowned by a modest steeple. The congregation was made up of hard-working people who either farmed or worked in the trades. Brother Russell, our minister, was a circuit preacher, so he served several churches in the area. That meant he only came through every other week. Before the service, the men always gathered outside to smoke a last cigarette before entering the service late—unless they were ushers. Ushers—and it was a high honor to be an usher—had to be on time. Week after week, each person returned to "their seat" in the pew.

One of the members of the congregation was an elderly man named "Dad Haggard"—or at least we were taught to refer to him that way. I have no idea how old he must have been, but I assume he was close to ninety. He always sat in the front pew because he was hard of hearing. When Brother Russell began to preach, Dad Haggard would take the receiver from his hearing aid and hold it at arm's length in order to better hear the sermon. We were told—all of us children at Pleasant Mound—that we must love Dad Haggard because he loved us. I don't remember any sign that he had any interest in us, much less loved us, but it was a dogma that we were to love him.

But then, as could only be expected, Dad Haggard died. The news of his death didn't make much of an impression on me until I found myself at the funeral. It was a hot summer day. I remember sitting with my father, who, even in the heat, wore a suit. I wasn't particularly bothered to be at the funeral. It seemed like just another worship service in which I was told to be quiet even though I was bored. But then I realized the whole congregation was lining up to see Dad Haggard for one last time. He lay in a casket that was positioned in front of the communion table, which bore the inscription "Do this in remembrance of me."

My father and mother got in line. As we drew close to the casket, my father suddenly picked me up so that I could look into it and see Dad Haggard's dead body. But I didn't want to. I didn't want to see death because I knew I'd begin to figure out that this meant that I would someday be dead too. A basic fact of life was sinking into my young consciousness. Still, when we got to the casket, I couldn't avoid looking at Dad Haggard. Much to my surprise, I had never seen him look better. The funeral home had done a wonderful make-up job, and his face had more color than it had ever had in life. There was also a red sash across his chest which proclaimed, in gold glitter, "Eternity is now." That's my first memory of death.

I'm not sure why I thought I should tell you this story. I think it's just my way of trying to give you some sense of who's writing these letters. I don't expect you to have any idea what it meant for me to be raised "Texan," but I at least hope to give you glimpses of that world by telling stories like this one. I do so because I loved and was loved by the people who constituted that world—a hard but wonderful world. Just think about the church name, Pleasant Mound. What kind of conditions existed that would lead people to give such a grand name to such an unimpressive, tree-covered rise? Or why would they call the small town in which I was raised Pleasant Grove? The answer is simple: in Texas, any small group of trees—and the trees were small—that gave you even brief relief from the sun was "pleasant." I expect most folk raised in England, that green land, would have found both places anything but pleasant.

You may well be thinking that I've forgotten I'm writing to commend to you the virtue of hope. But hope is what is grounded in the stories we tell. In particular, the hope I want to commend to you, the hope we should have as Christians, is a hope learned from a story about a death: the death of Jesus Christ. As Christians, we believe his death has everything to do with how we regard our own deaths. In his letter to the Romans, Paul writes,

> Therefore, since we are justified by faith, we have peace with God through our Lord Jesus Christ, through whom we have obtained access to this grace in which we stand; and we boast in our

hope of sharing the glory of God. And not only that, but we also boast in our sufferings, knowing that suffering produces endurance, and endurance produces character, and character produces hope, and hope does not disappoint us, because God's love has been poured into our hearts through the Holy Spirit that has been given to us. (Rom. 5:1–5)

That's quite a story to commend to a five-year-old. But I believe you'll discover its truth because God has created us to be hopeful creatures. The name we Christians give the story of creation and redemption is eschatology. Eschatology names a hope that defies frustrations by locating where we are in terms of an end which gives the present meaning. This is what Paul identifies as the great good news of the gospel—that we're included in this grand story of God's redemption. This is why Paul says that we can even hope to share the glory of God. The story of Christ's death and resurrection gives us hope, and hope is one of the virtues necessary for living into the story.

All this may sound quite "abstract" or "unreal," but your life is animated by hope. We literally cannot live without it. That may be why hope is often included in lists of the most important virtues. Many would, in fact, consider hope a more important vir-

tue than those I have commended to you in previous
letters—kindness, truthfulness, friendship, patience.
Oddly, these virtues are not numbered among either
the cardinal or the theological virtues.

Prudence (practical reason), courage, temperance,
and justice—these are usually identified as the cardinal virtues. They are given this name because many
think that they're primary, meaning that all the other
virtues depend on them. They're also called the "natural virtues" because many assume they're essential to
what it means to be human. The theological virtues
are faith, hope, and love. These are made possible by
the work of the Holy Spirit, and for that reason they
are not thought to be available to us naturally.

But I've always had problems with this way of di-
viding up the virtues. To contrast the natural virtues
with the theological can imply that the theological
virtues aren't "natural." But how can this be? As I've
tried to suggest in these letters, the virtues name the
habits we need to be the creatures we were created by
God to be. I also think it can be quite misleading to
identify the seven virtues above with *the* virtues. One
of the reasons I began my letters with "kindness" was
to suggest to you that some of the virtues that many
think aren't "primary" are in fact crucial for our living
well. Also, we need to remember that all the virtues
are interrelated. So, for example, we can't be appro-

priately courageous if we lack kindness. And hope without patience can tempt us to utopian fantasies.

Of course, I also began with kindness, truthfulness, friendship, and patience because I've tried to name and describe virtues that are correlative to your stage in life. Such a correlation may be artificial, but I do think the virtues are responses to needs and capacities we develop along the way. This finally brings me to the reason I chose hope as the virtue to commend to you on the fifth anniversary of your baptism: I hope to suggest that hope is the most "natural" of virtues because, as I've suggested, without hope we cannot live. Let me try to explain.

You are five, which is just another way to say you're sheer energy. And energy is the engine of hope. For example, that you have the energy to put your train tracks together every day in different configurations—that's hope. I've always loved G. K. Chesterton's account of how he came to see the world as charged with infinite energy. He observes that those who advocate "the towering materialism" of our day assume the world mimics a mechanism like a clock. Those who take a mechanistic view of the world like this think that if the universe was personal, it would vary from one minute to the next; it wouldn't entail repetition or be reliably predictable. But Chesterton counters this presumption:

It might be true that the sun rises regularly because he never gets tired of rising. His routine might be due, not to lifelessness, but to a rush of life. The thing I mean can be seen, for instance, in children, when they find some game or joke that they specially enjoy. A child kicks his legs rhythmically through excess, not absence, of life. Because children have abounding vitality, because they are in spirit fierce and free, therefore they want things repeated and unchanged. They always say, "Do it again"; and the grown-up person does it again until he is nearly dead. For grown-up people are not strong enough to exult in monotony. But perhaps God is strong enough to exult in monotony. It is possible that God says every morning "Do it again" to the sun; and every evening "Do it again" to the moon. It may not be automatic necessity that makes every daisy alike; it may be that God makes every daisy separately, but has never got tired of making them.

Chesterton says he always saw the world as magical, but he was educated to leave this view behind in the name of science. So he had to be re-educated by fairy tales to learn that the world can only truthfully be seen as a world of magic constituted by hope. If we live in a magical world, that must be because there is a magician. If there's a magician, there must be some purpose to the world; and if there's a purpose, then it makes sense to be a person of hope. Hope, then, is the virtue that makes possible our ability to recognize that the world in which we find ourselves has a story; and if there's a story, there's a storyteller. God, the storyteller, gives us hope by incorporating us into the story of creation, found in the beauty of each particular daisy.

Chesterton helps us see that there is an essential relationship between hope and the imagination. Because we are hopeful creatures, we're able to imagine that the way things are isn't the way things have to be. So hope means we can make demands on the world that may make our lives difficult. Because we're hopeful beings, we can hope to secure goods that we wouldn't even imagine could exist if we didn't have hope. Because we're hopeful, for example, we can

> *Hope, then, is the virtue that makes possible our ability to recognize that the world in which we find ourselves has a story; and if there's a story, there's a storyteller. God, the storyteller, gives us hope by incorporating us into the story of creation, found in the beauty of each particular daisy.*

hope to free the world of war. And we can hope to do so because we believe that through Christ the world has already been freed of war.

At this point it's extremely important to distinguish imagination from fantasy. For when our hopes are frustrated—and we have many hopes—we can be tempted to force the world to conform to desires not governed by the magic of God's good creation. So our hopes need to be schooled by the story of God, and language is crucial for such schooling. By this I mean that our ability to recognize the hopes that should shape our lives must be determined by a truthful story, one through which we learn to want the right things rightly. Naming the virtues permits an awareness we need to habituate those characteristics described as "hope" or "love."

Too often, optimism is confused with hope. Optimism is a general attitude that, interestingly enough, presumes that because I can't do much about my life, I can at least be "optimistic" in a vain attempt to make the most of a life I basically don't like. And I'm afraid our culture is more determined by optimism than by hope. That's why so many people try to protect themselves from the illusions that optimism can breed through cynicism. Cynicism is the form that hopelessness takes among a people who no longer believe they're part of a story that gives them hope.

Unlike optimism, hope is the habit that believes the arduous good is possible if we rightly learn patience. Faced with a difficulty, an optimistic person despairs, thinking there's nothing to be done. By contrast, a person of hope faces difficulty in a creative way by learning to improvise. Improvisation requires that we learn the skills of hope by attending to the stories of forebears who learned how to go on when it wasn't clear there was a way to go on. The stories of Israel and the Jews are particularly important for Christians as we learn again to live in a world in which we aren't in control. Of course, it was always an illusion to think we were in control. It's just our good fortune to live at a time when that illusion has been shattered. So if we are to survive as Christians, we must now learn to need one another.

We need each other because we cannot hope alone. We learn to hope by trusting others who have learned to hope by doing the same. Optimism is the attitude of those who isolate themselves from others, while hope is the virtue that takes pleasure in our need for others. It's often true that the imagination—on which hope depends, and which hope makes possible—also makes possible my discovery that I need others. For friends make my life rich with possibilities that I otherwise couldn't imagine.

Your energy means you cannot avoid being hopeful. The hopes you develop will provide you with still more energy to sustain new hopes. This means the hopes that are beginning to constitute your life will lead you to understand your life as a journey. In fact, hope is the name of the virtue that presumes life is a journey, a wonderful journey, through which we learn to ask much of ourselves and one another. To be on such a journey will require all the other virtues—in particular, patience and courage. Because to be a hopeful person means you rightly will want the world in which you find yourself to be a better one. I hope you'll want the world to be rid of war. But you'll have to be patient, courageous, and imaginative for that hope to be more than a fantasy.

The Kingdom of God is the name Christians give the journey on which hope sets us. It is a kingdom of hope in which we are taught to desire the good of all God's creation. It is a kingdom of peace in which we learn that the violence that can possess our lives is too often the result of despair fueled by fantasies of our own self-importance. People living in despair have no way to face death other than to deny death's reality or to have others die so that they might live. As a person

> *The Kingdom of God is the name Christians give the journey on which hope sets us.*

of hope in a world of despair, you may discover you'll have to suffer, but, as Scripture reminds us, through suffering you will learn to endure, and endurance produces character, and character produces hope.

Through your baptism you were incorporated into the life, death, and resurrection of Jesus. Through baptism you have been made part of a people who have faced down death, and death no longer has dominion over how they live. Death cannot defeat hope. If the story into which you were baptized was not true, then the hope into which you were baptized would be a cruel habit that could only lead to a life of frustration and despair. But that story is true, which means the energy pulsing through your life beckons you to a life of wonder and hope. For it turns out that eternity is now.

In the hope Christ makes possible,

Stan

Justice

Dear Laurie,

You're growing up in the South. "The South" is a mythical land constituted by a storied geography. "Mythical" doesn't mean that the South doesn't exist, but rather that the story that constitutes the geography doesn't quite fit the facts. The story is about war and a people who, against all odds, fought to sustain a questionable but honorable way of life. Slavery was the question that corrupted the heart of honor.

Justice, the virtue I write to commend on the sixth anniversary of your baptism, demanded the end of slavery. A horrible and terrible war was fought between "the North" and "the South" to bring it to an end. The reasons for the war may have been more complex than trying to end slavery in the name of justice, but there can be no doubt that if slavery hadn't existed, there wouldn't have been a war. Many people assume that if you desire a more just world, you can't exclude the possibility that some- where along the way you may need to kill someone. I hope to help you discover that those who love jus- tice—and I pray you will be one of them—do not and cannot go to war.

Justice seems like a "heavy" virtue. Images of jus- tice are often associated with old and serious people, usually men, who must make decisions of great con- sequence. Such decisions are usually those in which someone will have to suffer in order for justice to be done. This understanding of justice presumes, as Reinhold Niebuhr eloquently suggested, that often the best we can do is secure the fairest possible bal- ance of power between interest groups.

Justice so understood is particularly persuasive for those who live in America. America is a social order based on the assumption that the task of po- litical institutions is to secure agreements between people who share little in common other than the fear of death. That's why many Americans presume that a just society can be achieved without the people who make that society just. Because the prevailing thinking is that you can't trust people to be just, jus- tice is identified with procedural rules that can and must be enforced.

I fear that such an understanding fails to do justice to what it means to become a person of justice. Law is no doubt important for any account of justice, but justice is first and foremost a virtue. To be just requires that you be a person of good judgment. Judgment names the steady desire to see ourselves and others truthfully. Such seeing can tempt us to hate what we see because we can be disgusted by the smallness of our own and our neighbors' souls. That's why love must be at the heart of justice: to make possible our ability to accept that we have been forgiven and can forgive.

You may well think, "This is pretty heavy-duty stuff to lay on a six-year-old." And it is, just as growing up is pretty heavy-duty stuff. To grow up means you'll need to learn how to judge and be judged. In short, you'll need to learn to grow in wisdom. Wisdom entails learning to see and enjoy differences—differences as close and as far away as that creature called Stephanie. Such is the beginning of wisdom.

To be a human being—to be a son, a brother, a friend, a Southerner—means you can't avoid acquiring the habits necessary for you to be just. But to be a human being also means you can't avoid acquiring habits of injustice. Put another way, we often habituate injustices because we've assumed them to be "the way things are." We habituate injustice by failing to stop and ask, "Is this just?"

I am a Southerner. I grew up assuming that there were drinking fountains for whites and drinking fountains for African-Americans. I grew up assuming that whites went to white schools and African-Americans went to black schools. I grew up assuming that white people married white people and black people married black people. I grew up in a family that wasn't well-off, but still assumed that African-Americans only came into our small house by first knocking and then coming in through the back door. It never occurred to me to think that any of these arrangements were unjust. It never occurred to me that *I* might be unjust. That's because I simply saw these arrangements as "the way things are."

So justice is a way of seeing. To see justly entails a willingness to submit to the training necessary to see the world as it is. Some think this training is simply about learning certain rules—almost like learning the rules to a game; if everyone abides by the rules, then all runs smoothly. But it doesn't work that way because life isn't a game. There are

> *So justice is a way of seeing. To see justly entails a willingness to submit to the training necessary to see the world as it is.*

rules that can help, but often rules that at one time helped secure justice can now be used to sustain injustice. To treat everyone "the same," for example, can result in deep injustice. Justice requires an ability to see differences for the difference they should make.

The necessary training is learning to see the world redeemed by the cross and resurrection of Jesus. Jesus is God's justice. The church must be that justice for the world, for how else can we know that our lives are constituted by habits of injustice? If, for example, we share a common cup at Eucharist, how can we think we need one water fountain for whites and one for African-Americans?

> *The church must be God's justice for the world, for how else can we know that our lives are constituted by habits of injustice?*

One of my favorite poems is "As Kingfishers Catch Fire" by Gerard Manley Hopkins:

> As kingfishers catch fire, dragonflies draw flame;
> As tumbled over rim in roundy wells
> Stones ring; like each tucked string tells, each
>   hung bell's
> Bow swung finds tongue to fling out broad its
>   name;

Each mortal thing does one thing and the same:
Deals out that being indoors each one dwells;
Selves—goes itself; *myself* it speaks and spells,
Crying *What I do is me: for that I came.*

I say more: the just man justices;
Keeps grace: that keeps all his goings graces;
Acts in God's eye what in God's eye he is—
Christ. For Christ plays in ten thousand places,
Lovely in limbs, and lovely in eyes not his
To the Father through the features of men's faces.

"The just man justices" says everything and more that I have tried to say by commending to you the virtue of justice. Hopkins also reminds us that Christ is justice. The world's view of justice is an eye for an eye, and, accordingly, we all deserve death. But God doesn't play by those rules. God *is* justice, and only by looking to him can we know what justice looks like. God became one of us in Jesus Christ so that we might learn to be his justice for one another—and the world. That justice, a justice born of divine love, overflows our limits by making us more than we can imagine.

Justice born of love demands that the unjust be treated justly and with grace. I suspect that you, like me, will find that to be one of the most difficult challenges of being just. But we must remember that that is how God has treated us, making it possible for us to live at peace with our deepest enemy: ourselves. So it isn't true that if you desire peace you must first try to make the world more just, even if making the world more just means you must kill. To kill in the name of justice means such a justice cannot be the justice of God.

But I suspect that you won't be tempted to confuse the violence done in the name of justice with the justice that is Jesus. The challenges you'll face will be much more mundane. I began this letter by calling attention to "the South." I did so because you're being raised in the South and I am a Southerner. The racism that has gripped my life will also shape your habits, only in more subtle forms. You'll need help—just as I needed and continue to need help—to see the injustice racism names.

We are creatures determined to think well of ourselves. We don't want to acknowledge that we often fail to be just. We don't want to have the ways of injustice that shape the everyday revealed. So we're tempted to assume that the fact that some are unbelievably rich and some are destitute is just the "luck of the draw." Confronted by crises so desperate, we seem to think there's nothing just that can be done—and we're tempted to do nothing.

But the justice of Christ will help you resist those temptations. Remember that the justice of Christ will be shown through "the features of men's faces." You'll see injustice by seeing it on the faces of those whose features it distorts. When you see the faces of those who suffer, to be just will require you not to turn away. To be just requires learning how *to be with* rather than *to do for* those who suffer. To be just requires learning to see the ten thousand places where Christ plays. And to be just, you must learn to play there with Christ.

> *To be just requires learning to see the ten thousand places where Christ plays. And to be just, you must learn to play there with Christ.*

Love,

Stan

Courage

Seventh Anniversary: October 27, 2009

Dear Laurie,

Since I last wrote you, the world has changed. The economy has gone to hell in a handbasket. In the hopes for change, an African-American has been elected president of the United States. Of course, much also remains the same. America is still at war. The inequities that surround us continue to be assumed as givens by those of us who are rich. The sun comes up every morning, which means we still don't take seriously the warnings that we're confronting an ecological disaster. And yet, in truth, the world has changed.

That Barack Obama has been elected president is quite remarkable. His election doesn't mean that racism is no longer a problem for Americans, but it does suggest that America is becoming a different country. The difference may be, quite simply, that whiteness will no longer define what it means to be American. And that's a change that will take some getting used to—particularly by whites.

The financial downturn may prove even more challenging. We had assumed—Americans in particular had assumed—that economic growth was inevitable. We thought the economy would necessarily continue to expand to create more wealth. And, according to the related argument, such growth is crucial for the creation of a more nearly just society. Because if the rich get richer, there will be more to go around, making it possible to aid the poor without anyone having to sacrifice their own wealth. But then the bubble burst, and we discovered that much of our wealth was a fiction. That will take some getting used to.

The world, of course, is always changing. Some changes are more noticeable than others. In fact, it's probably true that the most important changes having long-term effect aren't even recognized. But the way things are never stays the same. So the problem isn't how to account for change, but how to remain constant in a world of change. To be constant, to be a person others can trust, requires the ability to change. To paraphrase John Henry Newman, it's important to change often, while remaining true to what makes you truthful. So, on the seventh anniversary of your baptism, I want to commend to you the virtue of courage, because it will require courage to be a truthful person.

As I've just suggested, courage isn't often associated with the challenge of negotiating changes in our lives while remaining constant. Usually courage is identified with dramatic and heroic acts. Though I certainly don't think it's a mistake that many associate courage with heroism, I want to propose to you that courage is an everyday virtue.

> *Usually courage is identified with dramatic and heroic acts. Though I certainly don't think it's a mistake that many associate courage with heroism, I want to propose to you that courage is an everyday virtue.*

The courageous usually don't think of themselves as intentionally heroic. That's because courage has been such an integral part of their lives that they seldom think they should "try" to be courageous. For instance, think of those who say "I was just doing my job" in response to being praised for a courageous act. That they respond this way seems right, because when confronted by a particular challenge, courageous people don't stop to think that they must act courageously. It follows that courageous people aren't usually aware of their courage or that they've done something courageous. Like most of the virtues, courage isn't something you try to have; instead, you discover after the fact that you have it.

If it seems odd to focus your attention on courage, that's because we most often associate courage with heroic acts, and society doesn't typically expect heroism of children. Even Thomas Aquinas states, "The virtue of courage is about the fear of dangers of death." Such fears just don't seem to apply to you at your age. Yet, death—and remember, you have been baptized—is no less a reality for you than for those of advanced age, like me.

Courage does have to do with fear and death. Aristotle, for example, thought courage was particularly exemplified by soldiers facing death in battle. He reasoned that soldiers couldn't avoid acknowledging that they might die in combat, but they would still do their duty. One very important note: Aristotle thought the courage exhibited by soldiers did not exclude but in fact required that they approach their possible deaths with appropriate fear. If they no longer feared death, then they weren't courageous—only foolhardy.

Aquinas follows Aristotle's account, but for Aquinas it's martyrs, not soldiers, who best exemplify courage. Martyrs, the ones who face death rather than renounce their faith, are the paradigms of courage. Like soldiers, martyrs are in a battle, but they fight not with weapons of steel but with patience and faith. This is why martyrs aren't considered heroes—because they don't try to defeat their enemy. Martyrs seek not to win but to endure.

You may now be thinking that my raising the possibility of martyrdom has little relevance for your life. Whatever your future may hold—and I hope you won't be called on to be a martyr—right now all you want to do is to grow up. But if I'm right that courage is an everyday virtue, then you'll find that to grow up well will entail your acquiring habits of courage. And those habits correspond to the kind of endurance that martyrs exhibit. Like the martyrs, you too will learn that it takes courage not to compromise the truth. In other words, you'll learn that courage requires vulnerability.

Talking about growing up is just a way of talking about what it means to have a passion for life. You'll discover that you'll be pulled into life by your passions, by your loves, and in the process you'll find yourself engaged with people and activities that, upon reflection, you might not have chosen if you had "played it safe." In fact, you'll often be frightened by what you've gotten yourself into. We're never very happy about being confronted by the unknowns we face as a result of our passions, because every unknown is a "little death." In your lifetime you'll face many unknowns, and you'll have to be courageous.

I've never thought of myself as being particularly courageous. But I have been writing a memoir, and friends tell me that takes a lot of courage. Though I'm not sure if they're right, I've discovered in the process of examining my life that I have from time to time been courageous. Let me be clear. I don't want to leave the wrong impression. I've lived a very protected, quiet life that has required little courage—at least, that's how it has seemed to me. But I have had thoughts that have required courage.

Courage has shaped my thinking because the way I think has been shaped by a passion for life. I'm not sure where that passion comes from, but I like to think that it's God-given. And even though my passion for life often gets me into trouble, I wouldn't live—I couldn't live—any other way. I've had to be courageous because of commitments I made before I knew what I was doing. Courage names the determination to see them through. This determination doesn't mean that the commitments don't undergo some transformations, but it does mean that they must be lived out.

> *Even though my passion for life often gets me into trouble, I wouldn't live—I couldn't live—any other way. I've had to be courageous because of commitments I made before I knew what I was doing. Courage names the determination to see them through.*

As I noted earlier, I had become convinced that the Crucifixion reveals a God who redeems nonviolently. This led me to blurt out, when asked by a friend, that "Yes, I am a pacifist." I had no idea what the declaration "I am a pacifist" would entail, not only for how I thought but also for how I lived. Living out my beginning declaration of pacifism no doubt involved a prideful desire to avoid having to acknowledge that I might have made a mistake, but I at least hope that something like courage was also involved. Because it takes some courage to be committed to living nonviolently.

I call attention to nonviolence because, as Aristotle's focus on war suggests, courage is so often associated with violence. Nonviolence is seldom thought to require courage, but to live without weapons requires great courage. Think, for example, of lives like those of Martin of Tours, Dorothy Day, and Martin Luther King. Their lives make clear that it takes immense courage to live nonviolently, and without lives like theirs, we literally couldn't imagine that an alternative to violence exists.

The courageous have fears the coward can never know, but those committed to living nonviolently have found a way to live without fear controlling their lives. Learning to live this way requires learning to draw on the courage shaped by the everyday.

Of course, by calling attention to nonviolence, I'm not so subtly suggesting that I hope that when you're older, you will also be a pacifist. But to focus on nonviolence may again seem to identify courage with the dramatic, the extraordinary rather than the everyday, and that's not my point. I think courage is also required for our ability to negotiate the more mundane aspects of our lives. And it is from the daily habits of courage that we are formed, eventually, into courageous people.

Your father has developed an account of everyday human relations that helps me show why and how I think courage is required in our everyday interactions. Drawing on lessons learned from the improvisational theater, he helps us see how often we're tempted to "block" conversation from going in directions that may make us vulnerable because of our fear of the unknown, which may be a threat to our assumed status. As an alternative, he suggests that we learn to "overaccept" attempts designed to block our interactions with one another—to refuse to be shut down. Improv actors only know how to say "yes."

According to your father, overaccepting requires that we see our lives in the light of a larger story. We fear that by doing so we will lose our integrity and identity. But overaccepting is actually a way to receive gifts that enable us to retain our identity without losing the passion for life. The larger story that makes such a way of life intelligible is called "gospel." God—at least the God we believe has been made known to us in Israel and in Jesus—refuses to destroy what God has made as a response to our rebellion. God refuses to let our sin undermine the salvation offered through Christ. Grace is one of the ways we describe what God's "overacceptance" means.

Because God has redeemed us, we can live dangerously. We can take the risk of nonviolence, trusting that is how God has chosen to reveal God's Kingdom. To live by overaccepting requires courage. Courage so understood is embodied in skills of speech and behavior that make imaginative alternatives possible. When you think about it, you realize you're already learning skills of overaccepting in school. "No" isn't a word often used in your Montessori classroom. You're learning to wait your turn to use the knot board by recognizing that waiting gives you the time to explore other options. The development of the habit called patience becomes a resource to sustain a life of courage that hopefully can be an alternative to violence.

The great trick will be how to make the courage you're acquiring in school, in your interactions with your parents, and even in your more challenging relations with your sister into a way of life. That will entail, as your father suggests, learning to live into the story into which you were baptized. To learn to do this requires that you be surrounded by friends who are courageous. You may be living in a time of diminishing material resources; you may be living at a time in which it is by no means clear how to negotiate "being white." But if you're surrounded by courageous friends, you'll discover that life isn't a zero-sum game. And you will likely discover courageous friends among those who have already learned to live truthfully in the face of poverty and loss of power. In some small way I hope I may be counted among the many friends you will need to learn to live courageously, that is, truthfully.

Peace and love,

Stan

Joy

Dear Laurie,

You're learning to play basketball. And you're not only learning to play, but it's clear that you love to play. I'm a witness. I went to one of your games, and I enjoyed watching you enjoy playing basketball. To learn to play this game is a wonderful way to acquire the virtues. Basketball requires doing the same thing over and over again in order to acquire the habits, the skills, necessary to do what seems quite simple but turns out to be quite difficult. I hope you'll discover as you grow up that the virtues have much in common with learning to dribble the ball well.

We seldom become virtuous by trying to acquire the virtues. Instead, the virtues ride on the back of compelling activities such as playing basketball. By learning to dribble the ball, you're acquiring habits that you'll discover are significant for learning to live happily. Basketball isn't the only way to learn the habits we associate with the virtues, but this game, particularly in North Carolina, is one of the "givens" that we have for making us better people. We need more than basketball to live well, but learning to play it isn't a bad place to start.

So on the eighth anniversary of your baptism, I want to commend joy to you as a crucial constituent of being virtuous. I do so because I think joy names the empowerment, the sense of satisfaction, that I hope you feel as you learn to play and watch basketball. But this is tricky, because although joy is crucial to being virtuous, joy itself is not a virtue. That's why I suggested that joy is an essential part of the virtues. I simply can't imagine commending the virtues to you without calling attention to the role that joy already plays, and I hope will increasingly play, in your life.

Being joyful isn't something we can try to be. Joy is spontaneous. It seems to come unexpectedly. For this reason, we think joy—because we can't anticipate when it will "show up"—must be more like an emotion than a habit. We associate joy with words like "ecstatic"– a word we seldom use to describe the virtues. We do say we should try to enjoy this game or this music, but even then we're not sure we know what we mean by the word "try." It seems that we're either joyful or we're not. So it makes little sense to tell someone they ought to be joyful.

Yet in Galatians 5:22–23 Paul includes joy in a list of the characteristics we associate with the virtues. He tells us that "the fruit of the Spirit is love, joy, peace, patience, kindness, generosity, faithfulness, gentleness, and self-control." Many have read this passage as a "grab bag" list of random character-istics that Paul commended to the Galatians. But there is a deep interconnection between these that is instructive for helping us understand why joy is on Paul's list. I think Paul would agree that the joy which comes from playing basketball isn't unrelated to the joy which comes from the Holy Spirit.

As Paul suggests, there's a strong relation between self-control and joy. People capable of joy don't fret over "being in control." They don't have to try to be in control because they're happy with who they are. And they feel this way because who they appear to be isn't different from who they are. It's not as if they must try to be people of faithfulness and people of integ-rity, because those things simply *flow* from who they have become because they do what they enjoy doing.

The other characteristics Paul includes wouldn't be possible without joy. Love is joy in the presence of the other; peace is the rest that joy makes possible; patience is the time that joy provides; kindness and generosity are the expression of the joyful reality that love isn't a zero-sum game; and gentleness is the response in joy to another's touch. Joy, in short, is made possible by the assurance that through the Holy Spirit we have been given a life worth living.

I hope this provides you with a very different perspective on morality than is often assumed today. Many associate being "moral" or "virtuous" with having to do what you don't want to do. "Having a good time" and "being good" are often assumed to name quite different modes of life. But if basketball isn't just an analogy for becoming good but is one of the ways we might actually become good, then the idea that morality is a burden has got to be wrong. What we ought to be, what we ought to do, shouldn't be different from what makes us happy. Of course, we may often have to make sacrifices to do what we know we should do if we are to be who we are. But there's a deep satisfaction that can come from having done what we know we have done rightly.

To call attention to the role joy plays in a life of virtue helps us remember that whatever else we may be, we are bodily creatures. The habits we acquire by learning to dribble the ball aren't the preconditions for our learning to think "basketball"; they're the thinking that *is* basketball. We don't think *with* our bodies, yet our bodies think. You've learned to dribble the ball not as an end in itself, but to be in a position to make a pass at the right time to the right player. Passing may even be a more complex skill than dribbling because it requires you to know well the habits of your teammates. This tells us something important: our bodies require that we rejoice in the existence of other bodies.

That we associate joy with feeling and emotion is surely right, indicating as it does the bodily character of the virtues. But we can "feel" joy when we shouldn't. Because we can get joy "wrong," some worry that joy shouldn't be considered essential to thinking about what it means for us to be good. Joy seems too much like a matter of taste. But being a virtuous person is to be a person of good taste. Good taste (contrary to our popular conception of it) isn't arbitrary or subjective; it's the formation of judgments about matters that matter. It's good taste to judge the way basketball is played at Duke to be superior to the way it's played at the University of North Carolina. That's why you rightly rejoice when Duke wins.

That joy and good taste are essential for our being people of virtue challenges the assumption by many that morality names only the most important and significant aspects of our lives. Morality does name these, but, as Aristotle suggested, that means how we amuse ourselves is significant. He also notes that it's important to listen and speak rightly when we meet people. And the company we keep will make a big difference in how we learn to do these things. This may remind you of an earlier letter I wrote in which I tried to show how friendship makes all the difference between the lives of the virtuous and the non-virtuous.

Aristotle even suggests that those who go to excessive lengths trying to raise laughs are acting like "vulgar buffoon[s]." For often the ones desperate to make others laugh aim to gain their approval in a way that causes pain to those who are victims of the jokes. Aristotle certainly thinks that jokes are a good thing, and that those who never joke are "boorish and stiff." But he also thinks it important to tell and listen to jokes in a manner befitting decent and civilized people.

There is in fact a connection between humor and joy. If joy is an essential part of the virtuous life, I find it hard to believe that a person of virtue can be devoid of humor because humor requires that we not take ourselves too seriously. Put differently, a person of virtue recognizes that their life is a gift made possible through the goods that make us more than we can be on our own.

Basketball, humor, and their relation to the virtues and joy may seem an odd set of associations on the eighth anniversary of your baptism. None of this has seemed straightforwardly Christian. I did call your attention to Paul's list in Galatians, but a list is just a list. And yet I think as you grow into your baptism, you'll discover that joy is at the heart of being a Christian. I hope you'll find it to be true that to be a person of virtue is to learn to rejoice in what we have been given. And to learn to rejoice in this is called "worship."

I find it interesting that Paul identifies the list in Galatians as "the fruit of the Spirit." He observes that there is no law against any of the characteristics he commends. He continues, "And those who belong to Christ Jesus have crucified the flesh with its passions and desires. If we live by the Spirit, let us also be guided by the Spirit. Let us not become conceited, competing against one another, envying one another." If the tack I've taken in this letter is right, when Christians live into their baptism, they cannot help but be a people of virtue and, for that reason, possessed by joy.

> *If the tack I've taken in this letter is right, when Christians live into their baptism, they cannot help but be a people of virtue and, for that reason, possessed by joy.*

Peace and love,

Stan

Simplicity

Dear Laurie,

Simplicity? Why in the world would I, on the ninth anniversary of your baptism, recommend to you simplicity? Simplicity doesn't often appear on lists of virtues. And that it isn't considered a virtue may tell us something important about the virtue tradition. The virtues are often thought to be characteristics of the strong, the intelligent, the well-off, the noble. But simplicity isn't usually a word used to describe these kinds of people. Yet I think that simplicity, particularly for any account of how the virtues work for Christians, must characterize our lives.

You're being raised in a world of privilege. The strong, the intelligent, the well-off, and the noble make up your everyday world. That you are so privileged is a good thing. And I'm part of the same world because I am also privileged: I spend my life reading books and writing. That I'm able to spend my life this way means I depend on a world made possible by people of power and wealth. Yet I like to think I remain a simple person, even though I know this could be an indication that I'm deeply self-deceived. And it's by no means clear what the relation may be between simplicity as a virtue and being a simple person.

That I've focused on simplicity at this time says more about me than you. As I grow older, I think often of my father. He was a simple man, a bricklayer, dedicated to God and his family. There was no deceit in him: what you saw was what you got. I like to think I'm not unlike my father. And I would hope that as you grow up, you'll be like my father. But you'll be told that people like him, simple people, were able to be simple because they lived in a time far less complex than the time we live in now.

"Complexity" isn't just a description used to characterize our time. "Complexity" is thought to be a good. We're told we live in a complex world that is beset with complex problems that defy simple solutions. So we need complex people who'll be able to handle these complex problems. In fact, the university where your mother and father work is an institution dedicated to producing complex people who will deal with such problems. Whether you like it or not, you're being raised in a university culture. The very fact that I'm your godfather writing these letters to you is an indication that you're destined to be "complex."

But I'm not at all convinced that my father's world was less complex than today's world. How could you possibly know if such a claim is true? As a child, my father rode a horse to school. As a young man, he adjusted to a world determined by the automobile. Every time and every world is complex in its own way. And for that reason, every time and every world require that we learn what it means to live simply. For the contrast to simplicity isn't complexity but pretention and artificiality.

It's tempting to think of simplicity as a virtue that derives from the desire to be authentic, but my father had no such desire. His simplicity was made possible by the very fact that he never desired to be anything other than what he had been given. Simplicity grows from the satisfaction of knowing

> *It's tempting to think of simplicity as a virtue that derives from the desire to be authentic. [But] simplicity grows from the satisfaction of knowing you want the right things rightly.*

you want the right things rightly. My father wanted good work that would make it possible for him to live as a Christian, a husband, and a father.

I grew up in the South in a time when people whom we now describe as "developmentally disabled" were called "simple." They were so called because it was assumed that they didn't possess the ability to achieve more than the basics of life. The description "simple" wasn't a compliment, but neither was it a negative characterization. To be simple was a description suggesting that whatever such a person lacked, they had the fundamentals right. That meant they knew how to love and to be loved. To know how to do this can be a very complex, demanding activity, which means, as I suggested, that simplicity doesn't exclude complexity.

But calling attention to the relation between simplicity and those who are simple is also important if the virtue tradition is to avoid being associated only with the privileged classes. Of course, this connection doesn't mean that the virtue of simplicity will be more easily acquired by the simple than those who aren't so characterized. Simplicity is but a mark of one's being at peace with who one is in relation to God and God's creation.

Simplicity is best understood as the virtue characteristic of those who don't have to try to be what they are. This is why simplicity may be a virtue that's a necessary characteristic of every other virtue. For example, the courageous must be courageous with simplicity, because without it they'll be tempted to "prove" their courage, which would make them foolhardy, not courageous. If simplicity is a virtue that qualifies every other virtue, this may be the reason it's often not listed among the virtues. But this observation implies that an account of simplicity is all the more important if we're to recognize the significance of simplicity for a well-lived life.

There is no doubt that simplicity resembles honesty and integrity. And robust accounts of these may seem to make it unnecessary to name simplicity as a virtue. But I think, particularly in the world in which we find ourselves, it's important that we not lose the significance of simplicity. Integrity and honesty without simplicity can be harsh, cruel virtues that are more like weapons against others than characteristics that build community.

How does one habituate simplicity? I suspect that simplicity derives from having good work to do. I don't think it accidental that my father was a bricklayer. He had good work to do not only because the work he did was good in itself, but because the work served goods that couldn't be achieved without it. Simplicity, the satisfaction that comes from a life of good work, is inherent in the unembarrassed declaration of your work when asked who you are or what you do. When my father said he was a bricklayer, he meant that how he laid bricks was no different from how he lived every minute of his life.

If we are to live lives of simplicity, the challenge we face is not that our world has grown more complex, but that our lives are increasingly compartmentalized. Many people assume that what they do in one aspect of their lives isn't connected or relevant to what they do in other aspects. This explains why some presume that what they do in their work isn't relevant to how they conduct their personal relations. The issue isn't simply that these different roles demand different skills; the issue is also moral. I can't be a person of simplicity and presume that what I do in one setting has no connection to what I do in others. That way of thinking is artificial and invites self-deception.

As you grow up, you'll find that the temptation to compartmentalize your life will be ever-present. In fact, it will be so powerful that you won't be able to notice that it's a temptation. To be able to compartmentalize our lives seems to be a necessary survival skill if we're to be "successful" in the world. The false distinction between the public and the private seems to be a "given" because it makes possible our presumption that we aren't "really" the person who has had to do in public what we wouldn't do in private. If you find yourself saying, "This isn't really me," that's an indication that the simplicity which should characterize your life is in jeopardy.

In the Sermon on the Mount in the Gospel of Matthew, Jesus tells his disciples that they shouldn't take oaths in the name of God. Instead, he says, we should simply let our "word be 'Yes, Yes' or 'No, No'; anything more than this comes from the evil one" (5:37). Clearly, plain speech and simplicity are deeply connected. (But it's also very important to remember that eloquence and plain speech are not incompatible.) You'll find that there's a profound beauty that radiates from those whose lives manifest simplicity. For those individuals have learned, as Jesus says in the Sermon on the Mount, and as the birds bear witness, that to trust in God makes possible a life that is otherwise impossible.

There's a lovely hymn written and sung by a rather strange group of Christians called the Shakers that expresses well the simplicity that comes from trusting God. It goes like this:

'Tis the gift to be simple, 'tis the gift to be free,
'Tis the gift to come down where we ought to be.
And when we find ourselves in the place just right,
'Twill be in the valley of love and delight.

When true simplicity is gained,
To bow and to bend we shan't be ashamed.
To turn, turn will be our delight,
'Till by turning, turning we come 'round right.

The Shakers rightly sing that simplicity is a gift. It is the gift of freedom manifest in people who rejoice in what they've been given. To have the gift of simplicity is to rejoice in the recognition of life as gift. And to be capable of such recognition makes possible a life that isn't overburdened by self-doubt, born from a self divided from itself. It is a gift, as the Shakers say, that comes from the sense that one's life has "come down" where it was meant to be. And those who delight in where their lives have "come down" enjoy the possibility of recognizing simplicity. They also have a fighting chance of avoiding the great enemy of simplicity—pretention.

To have the gift of simplicity is to rejoice in the recognition of life as gift. And to be capable of such recognition makes possible a life that isn't overburdened by self-doubt, born from a self divided from itself.

The Shakers thought they had to live simply if they were to have lives of simplicity. So they supported themselves by farming and making very simple furniture and implements. And they didn't marry, or have children. Not surprisingly, they didn't survive as a community, but their witness lives on. They represent a powerful challenge to the "complexity" of our lives because their lives manifested a joy that simplicity makes possible.

Life today is complex. And your life will be complex. But I hope and pray you'll discover that you've "come down where you ought to be." I hope and pray you'll discover simplicity.

Peace and love,

Stan

Constancy

Tenth Anniversary: October 27, 2012

Dear Laurie,

It was a sad going. You and your family have gone back to England. It was probably time for all of you to return. Your mother and father needed to return to serve the church in England. You and Stephie needed to return because if you had stayed much longer in America, I'm afraid you would be Americans. There's nothing wrong with being American, but your family is English. And the stories and habits that make you English need England if they're to flourish. So, though I dislike it, I'm happy for you that you've gone back to England. But I'll miss taking you to see Duke basketball games.

I told Paula that I was so overwhelmed by your family's leaving that I almost forgot it was time to write my annual letter to you. I asked her which virtue she thought I should recommend on the tenth anniversary of your baptism. Without naming a specific one, she suggested that it should be an English virtue. Now there's an intriguing thought—that there might be a virtue peculiar to a place. Aren't the virtues the same everywhere?

It's an extremely important question that, if properly addressed, would require more space than is appropriate for these letters. But the short answer, which is at least my answer, is that place and time do make a difference in how a specific virtue is understood. It may even be the case that a virtue that previously hasn't been named, or whose importance hasn't been recognized, may become central to a tradition. I believe the virtue of constancy is such a virtue.

Constancy may not be a virtue peculiar to the English people, but if the philosopher Alasdair MacIntyre is right, it's a virtue that has been best displayed in the novels of Jane Austen. His claim is even stronger because he argues that Austen is among the first to identify, as well as give an account of, constancy as a virtue. Constancy may not have been singled out in the past because persons of patience and courage often have characteristics we now associate with constancy. But in his book *After Virtue*, MacIntyre observes that Austen recognized that the increasing fragmentation of the social world required the naming of constancy as a virtue necessary to sustain the integrity of the self.

Courage and patience will shape how one is constant, but constancy is necessary for the way the courageous and patient person negotiates a world in which those two virtues lack exemplification. So by commending constancy I'm also trying to tempt you to read Jane Austen. Because isn't it true that reading Austen is one of the ways you become English? Of course, I hope you won't restrict your reading to Austen, but will also read at least some of the novels of Anthony Trollope.

Austen and Trollope were great "moralists" who wrote to help us live well, and constancy was as important to Trollope as it was to Austen. Both novelists associated constancy with what it meant to be a "gentleman." They knew some men might appear to be gentlemen but in a crisis couldn't be trusted to act as gentlemen should. True gentlemen would be constant. They would be what they seemed to be. Trollope also thought that forgiveness was crucial for being able to live a life of constancy. Because it is only by being willing to be forgiven that we can avoid telling ourselves false stories that finally result in deceptions that make it impossible for us to be constant. These are complex matters, which is one of the reasons I suspect the exploration of constancy is best done in novels and, in particular, the English novel.

So I hope that constancy is an "English virtue" because I myself am an unapologetic lover of England and, in particular, of Austen's literature—and Trollope's, too. Small wonder that it's one of my deepest wishes that you'll learn to love the English novel. And I hope you'll fall in love not only with Austen's and Trollope's books but also with the way of life they so lovingly portray in them. Both writers develop the kind of stories that make the English English.

The England of Austen and Trollope, of course, no longer exists. They assumed an established church that legitimated a socially stratified society. England is still socially stratified, only now the stratification is determined primarily by money. By directing your attention to Austen and Trollope, I'm not suggesting that you should want—or that it's even possible—to return to their world. What I am suggesting is that their understanding of constancy has become all the more important given the loss of the world they assumed. The church they knew is gone, but I think they help us imagine what kind of church and what kind of Christians we need to be if we are to be people of constancy.

I'm not calling your attention to constancy only because of its "Englishness." I think constancy is particularly important given your age. Soon you'll be a teenager. I have little idea what that will mean for you in specific ways, but I do know that you'll go through many changes. Your body will change, your friends will change, your interests will change, and your relation to your family will change. Yet through all those changes you'll need to remain Laurie Wells. Constancy is the virtue that makes possible "you being you" through the changes, changes that may be good or bad, that will constitute your life.

> *Constancy is the virtue that makes possible "you being you" through the changes, changes that may be good or bad, that will constitute your life.*

Understood this way, constancy is a virtue that is shaped by, as well as shapes, the times in which we live. We are creatures of time whose very lives constitute time. Constancy is the virtue—a virtue on which all the other virtues depend—that gives our lives coherence through the changes we must go through. Constancy reflects and gives expression to the narratives that give our lives coherence and unity. Put in more technical language, constancy is the virtue that is correlative to the purposive character of our lives.

Constancy is the form of a whole human life. But it may appear quite different from one person to another. For one thing, people have different temperaments. Some people are just "naturally" happy, and some are just "naturally" pensive. How constancy appears in a person who, for example, is never "down" may be quite different from how it appears in someone who may be described as "thoughtful." Constancy, in other words, makes us individuals without underwriting an individualistic ethic.

> *Constancy is, in short, the habit of "being me." A person of constancy can be trusted to be who they seem to be.*

Constancy is, in short, the habit of "being me." A person of constancy can be trusted to be who they seem to be. In this respect, there's deep connection between promise-keeping and being a person of constancy. To be constant means you can be counted on to keep your promises. That is surely part of what it means to be trustworthy, although I think being trustworthy also characterizes a life which is itself a promise that makes friendship possible. To be constant is to be a true friend. As you grow up, I think you'll find that to be that kind of friend, as well as to have friends who are constant, makes life worth living.

But this is no simple matter, because a person of constancy depends on the conventions of the time in which they live so they might be identified as a person to be trusted. Austen and Trollope assumed a society in which the way men and women related to one another was determined by well-understood conventions. It seems everyone knew what was expected of a lady or a gentleman. At first glance, that may seem to be an advantage in comparison to the ambiguous roles that mark our time. But in the world of Austen and Trollope a person could appear constant because they observed the conventions, while in fact the conventions made it possible for them to avoid being trustworthy. That's why Mac-Intyre suggests that the great enemy of constancy is charm, because charm too often makes it hard to distinguish someone who's genuine from someone who's just "going through the motions."

To become a person of true constancy, one must develop both self-knowledge and confidence in one's self to escape being determined by the opinion of others. I think this may well be the most important thing I have to tell you in this letter. You're entering a time in your life when you'll very much want to have the good opinion of your classmates—you'll very much want to be liked. This desire seems innocent enough, but it can also undermine constancy and what it means to be true to yourself. I think you'll discover that the kind of friends you have will make all the difference in becoming a person of constancy.

These are very tricky matters. To be constant means you can't let others determine who you are, and yet to become constant means you will rightly desire to be faithful to your convictions and those whom you trust and who trust you. Constancy, for example, means you can't let envy or resentment determine your life. If they do, then constancy has been displaced by the desire to be "known." Of course, it's a good thing to be known and loved by others. But when the desire to be known becomes an attempt to avoid loneliness, it can undermine constancy insofar as it often leads to desperation. When we become desperate, we can be sure we've forgotten who (and whose) we are.

So it makes all the difference what narrative shapes our understanding of constancy. Christians believe that we can be trusted to be who God has called us to be. We haven't been called to be self-sufficient. On the contrary, we've been called to be people who have learned we need the help of others if we're to be constant. To be Christian means we have been made part of a people who believe we owe one another the truth about ourselves. And finally, to be Christian means we aren't people marked by desperation. Together with the Psalmist we proclaim, "The Lord is my shepherd, I shall not want." Constancy is the virtue of gratitude and thanksgiving; we can be constant because Christ is trustworthy.

In The Great Thanksgiving of the Eucharist, the celebrant prays that the Holy Spirit will sanctify the gifts of the body and blood of Jesus. We continue the prayer by asking the Holy Spirit to "sanctify us also, that we may faithfully receive this Holy Sacrament, and serve you in unity, constancy, and peace; and at the last day bring us with all your saints into the joy of your eternal kingdom." I think it's no accident that in one of the most significant prayers we pray as a church, we ask the Holy Spirit to make us constant. And I'm sure that we do so because constancy, unity, and peace are God's gifts to us so that the world may

> *I think it's no accident that in one of the most significant prayers we pray as a church, we ask the Holy Spirit to make us constant. And I'm sure that we do so because constancy, unity, and peace are God's gifts to us so that the world may know that there's an alternative to the violence inherent in our fear of ourselves and one another.*

know that there's an alternative to the violence inherent in our fear of ourselves and one another.

It was a sad going. Paula and I feel your absence on a daily basis. Paula sees your house every day but knows you and your sister no longer live there. I feel the absence of your mother when I pass her vacant office in the Divinity School. We miss hearing your father preach. This "missing" reminds us that friendship is precious and never to be taken for granted. Distance makes a difference, but we have no idea what difference it will make for our friendships. What I do know is that God has given us the gift of constancy. That gift we give to one another, which makes possible our interconnectedness across time and space. We miss you, but we will, God willing, be your constant friends.

Peace and love,

Stan

Humility (and Humor)

⟫ Eleventh Anniversary: October 27, 2013 ⟪

Dear Laurie,

I usually begin these letters by trying to locate a time or a place that may serve as a marker for later reading. I refer to some event in the world or something that's happened in your life in an effort to acknowledge the passing of time. I'm going to do something a bit different in this letter: I'm going to write about where I am at this time and in this place. I've been a teacher for over forty-five years. A few years ago I realized I was tired of preparing for class, and I took that to be an indication that it was time for me to retire. So I will retire officially on June 30, 2014.

I'm often asked, "What are your plans in retirement?" The question usually makes me feel inadequate because the one asking the question usually assumes I ought to have some ideas about what I intend to do. But I don't have any plans. In fact, I've never lived my life according to a plan. I've just done what people have asked me to do. I don't see how retirement will change that set of habits—habits that go very deep indeed. That retirement doesn't seem to make that much difference to me is an indication of what a wonderful life I've been given.

There's another aspect of my life I want to mention that isn't unrelated to my retiring. I'm growing old. This probably seems like an odd remark, because you would think that growing old must be a reality that's hard to miss. But the habit of denial goes deep. I'm not sure, for example, if I have in any significant way acknowledged the fact that I'm getting old. Now I'm seventy-three. People say, "But you don't look seventy-three." That may be true, but my body certainly reminds me that I'm older than I look. I'm not complaining. It's just the way things are. Growing old is a gift because at the very least it gives you an opportunity to grow into death.

"To grow into death" is a phrase I'm not sure I should use in this letter because it suggests a "seriousness" that may seem inappropriate for someone as young as you. And at first blush it's a phrase that seems to have little to do with the virtue I want to commend to you on the eleventh anniversary of your baptism: humility. As I've said, retirement and growing old have reminded me in different ways of what a wonderful life I've been given. And humility is a habitual disposition that depends on gratitude for the lives we've been given. For that reason, humility, at least for Christians, is a virtue that must inform all the other virtues.

"At least for Christians" is a crucial phrase. In previous letters I've suggested how the identification of individual virtues and their relation to one another depends on the narratives that shape the fundamental practices of a people. For example, humility simply wasn't on Plato's or Aristotle's radar screen. They couldn't imagine a person of virtue who didn't demand from others recognition of their noble character and the honors they were due. From a Greek perspective, we would be less than virtuous if we failed to take pride in what we've become by what we've done. The Greeks simply didn't recognize any tension between egoism and altruism.

Platonism has certainly played a role in Christian thought. Augustine reports in his *Confessions* that the Platonists taught him to look for truth as something unembodied, and that was important because it allowed him to catch sight of God's invisibility. But that very achievement filled him with pride because he wished to be thought wise by other men. He confesses his knowledge was without charity because charity can only be built "on the firm foundation of humility, that is, on Jesus Christ." Augustine learned of his mistake by reading Saint Paul, who taught him that he who sees is able to do so only by the gift that has been given him by grace.

Augustine observes that the Platonists couldn't comprehend how God could become one of us to free us from our sin. But this ultimate expression of God's great humility is at the heart of what we believe as Christians. This means that who we are and what we believe are inseparable. We don't first believe and then become humbled; on the contrary, humility is the way we come to believe in Christ. That's why humility is such a central virtue for Christians.

One of the attractive aspects of Aristotle's ethics is his recognition that we're human beings and we shouldn't try to be more than human. Some Christians wrongly appeal to our humanity in an attempt to downplay our capacity to work out our salvation; we keep sinning because we just can't help ourselves. But redemption means that in Christ we see what it means to be human. And to be his disciples is to conform our lives to his. In doing so, we become more human—not more than human.

This has significant political implications, because too often persecution and even murder are justified by some for whom political passion is an attempt to make us more than human. Reinhold Niebuhr, the great political theologian, was right to emphasize the importance of humility for political engagement. Niebuhr's commendation of humility was primarily based on his criticism of the presumption of those who burn for justice, their error being that they too often forget that we seldom know what we're doing politically. Niebuhr was acutely critical of utopians for failing to recognize the complexity of politics. By contrast, the humility I'm suggesting as crucial to sustain a humane politics is one disciplined by discipleship: we are disciplined by following the One who humbled himself by becoming one of us.

But, as important as humility is for Christians, it's an odd virtue because the very character of humility means that if you must try to be humble, you probably don't possess the virtue of humility. The declaration "I am humble" turns out to be a self-contradiction. Those who are genuinely humble often don't call attention to themselves because their humility doesn't allow them to do so. They don't mind not being singled out for their humility because they're at home with who they are. They live in a manner that suggests they have nothing to prove. After all, humility is a virtue that makes it possible for us to rest easy with ourselves. This doesn't mean that humble people are self-satisfied. It means they live by acknowledging the gifts that have made them who they are.

Humility, like many of the other virtues, rides on the back of practices that are so captivating that we don't notice what we've become through the engagements we've undertaken. I've emphasized the Christological context that makes humility so important for Christians, but it's also important to recognize that our lives are constituted by everyday work that helps us discover, without our trying to be humble, that humility is derived from the good work we've been given.

> *Humility, like many of the other virtues, rides on the back of practices that are so captivating that we don't notice what we've become through the engagements we've undertaken.*

Think about how learning Latin requires you to submit to learning a grammar that's quite different from English grammar. The discipline required to learn a language may not make us appropriately humble in every aspect of our lives, but it can give us indications of how humility becomes a habit, shaping our desires and judgments. Learning Latin is hard work, and you should rightly be gratified when you've done the work necessary to show you understand the language. But you must also be grateful for those who show you how it's done. At the heart of gratitude is the acknowledgment that even that which we do is, as Augustine suggested, a gift.

I suspect that most of us don't think about being humble, though we assume at certain times we'll know how to express appropriate humility: "I couldn't have been so successful without the support of my _____." It's also possible to have the virtue of humility and yet have expectations of others such that we deny their humanity. We may well have the virtue, but pride is a subtle vice that makes it very hard to know if we have the self-knowledge that humility requires. I once asked a friend, who's a Roman Catholic priest in Ireland, if he thought the church might learn some humility in the face of the scandal surrounding the sexual behavior of some priests. He responded, "Possibly, because there is no humility without humiliation"—a claim that's probably too strong, but indicates how determinatively pride grips and how our lives as Christians, consequently, depend on being jolted out of our self-satisfaction sometimes.

There are imitations of humility that are important to distinguish from true humility. For example, it's a mistake to associate humility with self-effacement. There's a wonderful story about the great architect

Frank Lloyd Wright that suggests why humility isn't the same as not taking yourself seriously. A roof on a house Wright had designed leaked, so the owners took him to court to sue him for what they took to be a faulty design. Wright was put on the stand and asked to identify himself. He declared, "I am Frank Lloyd Wright, the world's greatest architect."

After Wright gave his testimony, he returned to the table where his lawyer was sitting. He expressed his dismay at what seemed to be Wright's overestimation of himself. His lawyer pointed out that the jury couldn't help but think Wright was arrogant, and that wouldn't help in his defense. Wright responded, "What could I do? I was under oath. I had to tell the truth." Although Wright wasn't generally a person of humility, he rightly understood that humility and truthfulness can't be separated. Humility requires a truthful assessment of who we are as well as an appropriate regard for ourselves.

So truthful self-knowledge is at the heart of the virtue of humility. I'm not suggesting that the person of humility must be an intellectual. Augustine saw that hard-won knowledge could engender a form of pride. By contrast, he thought the virtue of humility depended on the recognition that one can only do what one has received. As I've suggested, people who are genuinely humble are at ease with themselves.

They're the kind of people that others look forward to being with because they enjoy what each person brings to the interaction. Their humility is an invitation for others to join in common tasks for the common good.

That humility is a virtue that makes possible a common life suggests that there's an essential relationship between humor and humility. It's often thought that a person of humility is someone who's able to laugh at themselves. There may be something to that, but I think the relation between humor and humility is much more profound. Ted Cohen, in a wonderful book entitled *Jokes: Philosophical Thoughts on Joking Matters*, observes that when a joke has been successful, a feeling of satisfaction unites the teller and the hearer because they recognize that the joke joins them in a common world. In particular, a joke depends on much that is unsaid; it is only in the telling of the joke that we recognize what we have in common, and this is expressed by the laughter we share.

Cohen uses the term "intimacy" to describe what happens when a joke has elicited a shared response. The intimacy a joke both presupposes and creates is a sense of community constituted by a shared set of beliefs, dispositions, prejudices, preferences, and feelings. For that reason, telling a joke suggests that the teller wants to reach another in the hope that the two can better understand one another. The point is that jokes help us recognize we're not so different that we can't discover some commonalities.

I'm calling your attention to the importance of humor for the virtue of humility because you're reaching the age when children often use what they think of as humor as a form of cruelty. Jokes can be used to denigrate other human beings who aren't in a position to defend themselves. For example, I suspect you'll discover as you grow up that, given the need young people often feel to establish who's "in" and who's "out," derogatory humor will be used against those who are "out." This explains the use of jokes that stereotype people in England who are allegedly "immigrants." The need to use humor as a weapon indicates that those telling the jokes are deeply insecure.

Of course, the relation between humility and humor is a "loose" one. A person of humility isn't necessarily a person who has a sense of humor. The phrase "to have a sense of humor" suggests that by nature you either have such a sense or you don't. Similarly, I suspect some think that humility is a disposition that just comes naturally to some people and not to others. It's understandable that some might consider both these characteristics to be "natural" because, as I've suggested, to try to be humble seems self-contradictory. So does working hard to be funny. People who try desperately to be amusing often make painful companions.

Still, humility and humor are acquired habits that are essential to a well-lived life. I suspect I'm primarily focused on humility in this letter because I also wanted to direct your attention to humor. It's well-known that humility is seldom associated with children because it's assumed you haven't lived long enough to have a life that threatens to be prideful. But I'm not sure that such an assumption is right. I suspect that pride threatens the life of the young just as much as the life of older folk like me. I've called attention to the relation of humility and humor because I hope their communal character can help you develop the kind of self-knowledge on which they both depend.

Which finally brings me back to where I began (he says in all humility)—with me. I'm told that I am a humble person. I don't know if that's true or not. But it is true that in the world of academia those who have written as much as I have assume they've been granted the right to take themselves very seriously and to expect others to take them as seriously as they take themselves. I myself have never been able to develop that sense of importance.

I suspect that my not being able to take myself that seriously is partly due to my background. Coming from the working classes, I've always distrusted those in the higher, knowledgeable classes who presume they're better than those who work with their hands. So I can't credit my refusal to claim my due as a successful academic to possessing the virtue of humility. It's probably due more to my resentment of those who don't know what it means to have to work hard at hard work in order to survive.

I also suspect that my "humility" is an expression of my sense that I probably don't belong in the world I've inhabited for most of my life—the world of the university. I've never felt I acquired the scholarly skills early on to do the kind of work that distinguished academics do. So I always feel as if I need to learn—something that's worked out well for me, because that drive has helped me stay ahead of the game in my field. Yet insecurity isn't the same as humility. Put differently: a humility that expresses a more fundamental insecurity isn't humility.

But I've had a wonderful life. I've been given good work to do, and I've been given good friends to be with me in that work. So if I do have the virtue of humility in some small way, I hope it draws on a profound sense of gratitude for the life I've been given. For that life has given me the opportunity

I've had a wonderful life. I've been given good work to do, and I've been given good friends to be with me in that work. So if I do have the virtue of humility in some small way, I hope it draws on a profound sense of gratitude for the life I've been given.

to read Augustine, who directs me to the Savior, whose desire it is that we would be people of humility. How wonderful it is to have a life that makes possible a glimpse of the truth. It humbles me.

I've written to you in a manner that assumes you're growing up. You'll need to ask, "Why do I need to read Augustine?" And that's why I'm not apologizing for writing at a higher level. It's my way of recognizing that you're now acquiring the skills to ask such a question. I can only wish that your life will be as enjoyable as my life has been. We have both been very "lucky." May we never take that for granted.

Peace and love,

Stan

Temperance

Dear Laurie,

Time passes—quickly. At least for me it feels like time passes quickly. I find it hard to believe that I'll soon be seventy-four. And I find it hard to believe that you'll soon be a teenager. You have a life before you; I have a life behind me. By saying that, I don't mean to suggest that I don't still have some living to do. I certainly hope I have a good deal of living left, but that will no doubt be determined by the life I've lived. This truism doesn't seem all that interesting, but I think it's not irrelevant for the virtue I want to commend to you on the twelfth anniversary of your baptism: temperance.

You must find it odd for me to commend the virtue of temperance at this point in your life. You're just twelve years old. I suspect most people would think you're not old enough—yet—to need the virtue of temperance. But I suspect we need the virtues at every stage of our lives, although it's no doubt true that the virtues may look different relative to our age. I'm sure, for example, that being a person of temperance means something different to me now than it did when I was thirty.

Yet I think you'll soon find that one of the most difficult questions you'll be asked is "What do you want?" We assume that we know what we want, but I think that assumption is often quite mistaken. Our lives are carried along by the routines of the everyday, and that isn't a bad thing, but to have our lives so determined may be a way to avoid asking ourselves what we really want. Temperance is relevant here because it's the virtue that shapes our wants. Let me try to explain that strange observation.

Temperance is the virtue made necessary by the fact that our lives are constituted by desire. It's easy to miss this fact because we find it hard to acknowledge what makes us who we are—it's so close to us that we can fail to comprehend what really makes us tick. For instance, we seldom notice that we want to live because that's a constant, fundamental desire.

We also seldom notice how the most basic things we do reflect our desire to live. Eating is one of those things, and it's often been seen as one of the aspects of our lives that should manifest temperance. Eating is so basic, in fact, that when I'm asked, "Why should I be moral?" I reply, "Do you like to eat?" We need to eat, and that need pulls us into life with all of its complexities and pleasures. What should I eat? How often should I eat? How much should I eat? A temperate person must take pleasure and enjoyment in eating the right things rightly.

I emphasize the importance of temperance in the formation of desire because temperance is often associated with the suppression or denial of desire. That's particularly true in some forms of Christianity, and most often those forms associated, no doubt unfairly, with the Puritans. This explains why the word "puritanical" is used to describe people who think it's wrong to take pleasure in anything. People so described are thought to believe that they need to be *in control of* their passions and desires. Though such people are often ridiculed, they're quite right to suggest that when the passions are disordered, our lives can go to seed more quickly than we can imagine. But the language of control has the disadvantage of suggesting that desires must be suppressed rather than formed by the virtue of temperance. There's a big difference between control and formation, and it's crucial to understand it.

In fact, the problem with the presumption that our passions must be subject to our control is that it usually leads to the unfortunate outcome that our desires control us. We can't control our desires simply by trying, through sheer will, to wield control over the world. That attempt is based on fear, and succumbing to fear will always weaken faith and the life of virtue. Instead, Christians must learn what it means to live faithfully—virtuously—even when we're not in control. This is why loving God and loving our neighbor is at the heart of what it means to be Christian. To love and to be loved means we're not in control, which can be frightening. Temperance is the virtue that defeats our fears by making possible our desire for friendship and community. It is the wisdom that enables us to face the fears that would threaten our peaceful relations with one another.

I've been told that in the Jewish tradition, the rabbis say that God will judge harshly those who haven't enjoyed every legitimate pleasure. Of course, everything depends on what's considered a legitimate pleasure, but I think the rabbis' statement is a good expression of how temperance is best understood. To be temperate is to take pleasure and enjoyment in what should give us pleasure and enjoyment.

Of course, desire isn't just wanting this or that; as I've suggested, desire is but another name for life itself. Aristotle suggests this is the case by beginning his *Nicomachean Ethics* with the observation that all people desire to be happy. After providing a list of what many people mistakenly think would make them happy, Aristotle argues, I think rightly, that a happy life is one of complete virtue in a complete life. We desire to be happy, but according to Aristotle that desire must be schooled by the virtues and, in particular, the virtue of temperance, because it's the virtue that habituates us to want the right things rightly.

Aristotle's understanding has influenced many Christian accounts of what it means to desire to be happy. But for Christians this desire entails more than Aristotle had the means to imagine. For Christians the desire to be happy can only be satisfied by our desire for God. We have been created for the enjoyment of God, who would have us as friends. What it means to enjoy God is, quite simply, to acknowledge that God takes joy in us, making possible our enjoyment of God. We love the Lord because he first loved us and made us in reflection of his glory. Temperance is the virtue that makes possible our enjoyment of God without reservation.

For Christians, the desire to be happy is perhaps best understood as our desire to be loved. We were created by love and we can die, psychologically and literally, if we find ourselves incapable of being loved as well as loving another. Love may be the most basic desire we know. Life itself wouldn't be worth living without its demands. Yet the desire to love and to be loved can make us miserable because we so often get it wrong. We too often love the wrong people wrongly and don't love those who are rightly to be loved. Temperance, the virtue often misunderstood as robbing us of joy, is the virtue that forms us to love the right things rightly.

That temperance is so important for a well-lived life is one of the reasons it's always listed as one of the cardinal virtues. I've never been convinced that prudence, courage, temperance, and justice are more basic than a virtue such as patience. But the importance of temperance for our living well cannot be denied. In particular, temperance, at least for Aristotle, is crucial for our ability to make intelligent decisions and judgments. In short, temperance is necessary for practical reasons because we often fail to make right judgments if we're under the spell of mistaken wants or unruly passions. It's also true that to acquire the habits that make us temperate requires that our lives be governed by our reason. But it's important to remember that reason itself is a form of desire—a reminder that everything is connected in a well-lived life.

I began this letter by observing that you'll soon discover one of the most demanding questions you'll be asked is "What do you want?" That question seems straightforward, like one we ought to be able to answer without a great deal of reflection. But you'll find that it's a very challenging question, because it isn't at all clear that most of us know what we really want. As a result, we often mischaracterize it, and the result is a misshapen life. Temperance is the virtue that gives us the time to discover what we want when our desires are rightly formed. Like many of the virtues I've recommended to you, temperance becomes a habit through our pursuing activities that are so compelling that we don't notice we're acquiring the patience necessary for our ability to want the right things rightly.

Like many of the virtues I've recommended to you, temperance becomes a habit through our pursuing activities that are so compelling that we don't notice we're acquiring the patience necessary for our ability to want the right things rightly.

I think one of the reasons I wanted to call your attention to temperance as you approach your teens is that I have a sense that those who are young float on a sea of desires. They want so many "things," and they seem to think that they must have what they want. But what they often want may have less to do with the object of their want and more to do with their simply wanting what a friend has. Endless copy-cat consuming becomes their way to sustain their relations with one another. For them, community means they desire the same things. And there are many people who are more than ready to exploit young people's attempts to discover who they are by what they buy. Temperance is the virtue that I hope will give you some ways to resist the insidious consumer ethos that suggests community is about owning similar things.

I have a friend, a philosopher, named Alasdair MacIntyre who wrote a wonderful essay on the understanding of temperance in Aristotle. MacIntyre argued that if we were formed by *sophrosyne*, the Greek word for temperance, we would discover that much of what we think we want is but an expression of greed. So if we embodied the virtue of temperance, it might well mean we would need to learn to accept a lower standard of living. MacIntyre's observation is important because it makes clear that temperance entails a politics and an economics that can hardly be comprehended in the world as we know it.

I began this letter by calling attention to our very different stages in life. I did so to suggest that you'll soon find yourself confronted by the question "What do you want?" Even more demanding will be the question "What do you want to get out of life?" Temperance means you don't have to answer those questions before you're ready.

But these are questions I too am asked and must also ask myself. What do I want as I grow old? Like it or not—and in general, I don't like it— I'm growing old. For me, that means I don't have the energy or the strength I did just ten years ago. My body has more pains than I

> *You'll soon find yourself confronted by the question "What do you want?" Even more demanding will be the question "What do you want to get out of life?" Temperance means you don't have to answer those questions before you're ready.*

care to acknowledge. I can no longer run, and I find exercising more difficult. Again, I'm not complaining. I'm only trying to describe the way things are.

So, in the face of growing old, what do I want? I've had a very full life, so what could I possibly want or desire when I'm seventy-four? I want as long as possible to cut the grass in my yard. How's that for an ambition? But mowing the lawn is physically satisfying work. When I've finished, I can look at what

I've done and think to myself, "This looks pretty good." I take this to be a good example of how important the body is for the formation of our desires: habits are bodily, and desires are bodily. Mowing the lawn covers a host of things I continue to want to do, but they're not the most important thing I want.

I've been the most fortunate of people. I've been given useful things to do by being a husband, father, teacher, and friend. And what I most want now, what I most desire, is to continue to be of use. If I can be, I should like to think that I'll play some role in God's good care of his creation. I've never considered myself to be a paragon of the virtue of temperance, but as I draw nearer to the end, I hope what I desire may in some way exemplify what it means to have loved God without reserve. I can only wish that you will have a life as full of passion and desire as I have had.

> *I've been the most fortunate of people. I've been given useful things to do by being a husband, father, teacher, and friend. And what I most want now, what I most desire, is to continue to be of use.*

Peace and love,

Stan

Generosity

Dear Laurie,

It's been some time since we parted company. You and your family have been gone for over three years. I still miss y'all (I use the Southern expression) terribly. Your father and I try to keep up by calling each other from time to time. He often tells me about you and the work you're doing in school. But that's not enough for me to know how to "picture" you. I'm sure I'd be quite surprised by how you've grown both physically and intellectually. That I have trouble picturing you makes it hard to know how to write more specifically as I commend to you the virtue of generosity. But as I will explain below, one of the reasons I thought generosity might be appropriate to commend now is that this virtue should make it possible for us to comprehend each other's lives even when we're not in close physical contact.

But before I say more about generosity, let me say a little about my life. I've been retired now for two years, but I can't seem to get the hang of it. Or, perhaps better put, I keep asking myself, "If I'm retired, why do I have all these deadlines to meet?" The answer is that I just can't say "no." So my inability to know how to retire is my own fault. But I'll keep working on it. It seems like something I should be able to do, but we are strange beasts, opaque to ourselves. I keep thinking, for example, "When am I going to grow up, and how will I know it when I have?" After all, I'm seventy-four. Surely that must mean something.

It's been a good year, but the death of Eden, our eighteen-year-old cat, made Paula and me very sad. She was a lovely cat who was smart and had a winning personality. Eighteen is quite old for a cat, because as they age, their kidneys start to fail. And her kidneys did give out, but even then she put up a struggle to live. It was if she was saying, "You have loved me, and I love you. I don't want to leave you." I strongly identified with how she fought death because I recognize that I'm no longer young, either. Death, I'm beginning to realize, isn't a theoretical possibility but a reality—even for me. Eden's brother,

Enda, is still alive, but he does everything very, very slowly.

I mention the cats because I think their lives can help us learn and manifest what it means to be generous. Animals may be "naturally" generous in their desire to share their lives with us, but that they are so doesn't lessen the significance of their generosity. I'm sure, for example, that you continue to remember the generosity of that wonderful dog called Connie.

We, of course, are also animals, and so are "naturally" generous. But for us to be naturally generous isn't quite the same as it is for dogs or cats. The problem with being this way is that when we don't have to work at being generous, we may fail to be generous in a manner that we and others can rely on. So the question becomes, What kind of work can we undertake to transform our natural tendency to be generous into a habit that makes us who we are? I imagine that every culture has some acts that are thought to be acts of generosity, such as giving aid to the poor. But, although this is certainly a good thing to do, it won't insure that the giver is in fact a generous person.

That we don't necessarily become generous by doing acts of generosity is an indication that we need to think hard about what it means to be generous. To be a generous person certainly will manifest itself in gen-

erous acts, but generosity is a virtue that's more fundamental than the giving of gifts. To be generous is to
have a disposition toward life and in particular toward
other people that's welcoming. A generous person is a

A generous person is a person of hospitality who is ready to share their life with others but also, and even more important, to have others share their lives with them. This isn't easily done because to welcome the stranger, who may be as near to us as a sister, a parent, or a spouse, threatens our ideas about ourselves and our own generosity.

person of hospitality who
is ready to share their life
with others but also, and
even more important, to
have others share their lives
with them. This isn't easily
done because to welcome
the stranger, who may be as
near to us as a sister, a parent, or a spouse, threatens
our ideas about ourselves
and our own generosity.

That's why generosity
depends on great drafts
of courage. Courage is
required because our lives
are so often ruled by un-
acknowledged fears. It's
particularly important to
recognize this because
when we do acknowledge our fears, our sense of
who we are might be called into question. When
we can courageously face these fears and determine

who we truly are, we can be truly generous. So a generous person is a person of courage; that courage helps them possess what might be called critical confidence in themselves to live life well. Such a person will manifest a knowledge of who they are in a manner that makes possible the risk of learning to know the other.

So what I'm proposing is that you think of generosity as the capacity to participate imaginatively in the experience, the life, of others. A generous person might be thought to be empathetic. I'm sure that empathy is one of the results that generosity may produce, but generosity is more basic than empathy. An empathetic person isn't necessarily generous, but a generous person may and probably will be empathetic. A generous person has the capacity to give themselves to others without any calculations of what they'll get in return.

> *Think of generosity as the capacity to participate imaginatively in the experience, the life, of others.*

I think it's quite easy to miss how pervasive and significant generosity is in our lives. For example, I think generosity is present when a writer gives us the gift of a narrative in which they invite us to enter into the life of another. Novelists often observe that the characters they create "get away from them" and do things they hadn't planned. An author's experiencing the inability to control their own creation is but an exemplification of life itself. Generosity is the virtue that puts us out of control just enough that we are open to the lives of others. And some of those "others" will be dogs and cats.

If writers are trained to be generous through the creation of characters, the very act of our reading what they've written may be one of the ways we learn to be generous. To read is to be pulled out of ourselves, to imagine a different life. The great enemy of generosity isn't selfishness. No, the great enemy of generosity is narcissism. And it's so much more difficult to counter precisely because it so completely possesses us.

You may have noticed that I've said nothing about generosity as a Christian virtue, yet I believe generosity is at the very heart of what it means to be Christian. But I'm assuming that what I've said about generosity might also be illuminating for those who aren't Christian. That this is true shouldn't be surprising to Christians because we believe our God is a generous Lord who loves those who don't acknowledge him no less than he loves us. The very act of creation is an act of generosity that brings into existence each person, and each with the vocation to participate in the love that sustains all that is.

Nowhere is the significance of generosity for Christians made clearer than in the Apostle Paul's Second Letter to the Corinthians. The church in Corinth was, as the church has continued to be, a mess. From Paul's perspective, the Corinthians were determined to engage in behaviors that were sure to offend God. But in Paul's second letter to them, he commends their repentance. He continues by reflecting on the importance of generosity in the hope that he can persuade them to give support to the poor in the church in Jerusalem. In particular, he holds up for the Corinthians the example of the believers in the churches of Macedonia, "for during a severe ordeal of affliction, their abundant joy and their extreme poverty have overflowed in a wealth of generosity on their part" (2 Cor. 8:2).

What's fascinating about this passage is Paul's association of the extreme poverty of the Macedonian Christians with their "wealth of generosity." What Paul presupposes is that generosity isn't simply what's to be given out of surplus. The Macedonians were very poor. According to Paul, their generosity was made possible because "they gave themselves first to the Lord and, by the will of God, to us." Paul, drawing on this example, then commends those in the Corinthian church to "excel in this generous undertaking" (2 Cor. 8:5, 7).

But Paul immediately says that he isn't commanding the Corinthian Christians to give to support the church in Jerusalem. Instead, he's testing the genuine character of their love. For, he says, "you know the generous act of our Lord Jesus Christ, that though he was rich, yet for your sakes he became poor, so that by his poverty you might become rich" (2 Cor. 8:9). Here I believe we have one of the most powerful articulations of what would become known as the doctrine of the Incarnation. For our sake, he who is rich, who is fully God, became for us fully human so that we might not be ruled by fear. For to be ruled by fear makes us turn in on ourselves in a manner that makes us isolated and lonely. The Incarnation is the generosity of God that overwhelms this loneliness.

That we are the creatures of such a God, a God who would become one of us, means we are a people who believe that we do not live in a world dominated by scarcity. Our Lord is a Lord of abundance whose love of the other makes our love of another possible. We're able to give (and receive) because we've been given all we need to be generous. When our gifts are received at the altar, the priest often says, "All things come of thee, O Lord," and we respond, "And of thy own have we given thee." A brief exchange that says everything that needs to be said: we can only give what we have been given.

As I've suggested, this is a remarkable passage in Paul's letter because we see the strong connection he draws between the generosity of the Incarnation and what it means for us to be a people of generosity. Paul tries to persuade the Corinthians to perform acts of mercy, but he presumes that such acts must reflect selves that are fundamentally generous. By "fundamentally" I mean that we are to be people of the gift. This means we are to be not only a people who are able to act generously, but also a generous people ready to receive the gifts of others. And we can never forget that we often are ill-prepared to receive such gifts because they challenge our need to be in control.

In this letter I've taken the liberty of writing at a more demanding level than usual. I don't mean that what I've written in the past is simplistic, but that I believe you'll soon be ready for this level of writing and thinking. You're still young but soon will be older. And as you grow older, you'll discover the complex challenges we call "being an

> *Many generous people have made your life possible. Don't be afraid of imitating them.*

adult." If I have any advice, it is simply this. Many generous people have made your life possible. Don't be afraid of imitating them.

Peace and love,

Stan

Faith

Fourteenth Anniversary: October 27, 2016

Dear Laurie,

I think it's been more than a year since we've seen one another. But your mom and dad give me frequent news about you. For one thing, I know that you're now in boarding school and that you're quite happy to be there. I'm happy to hear it. That you made the transition from home to school is a great thing. I have to confess, though, that I have little idea what it may mean to attend a boarding school, and even less what it might mean to do so in England. All I know about boarding schools is what I read in English novels. Their depiction of life in these circumstances is often one that suggests a pattern of cruelty, but I'm glad that doesn't seem to be true of your school.

As you know, I grew up in a working-class family. That meant I had no idea what a boarding school might be. In fact, while growing up I never heard anyone refer to one. I mention this to indicate what different worlds you and I come from. In the past I've called attention to our difference in age, but it's not only that which creates difference but also our place in the world. That we come from such different places is neither good nor bad but simply the way things are. I remain hopeful that we can still communicate well. After all, my father and I were able to understand one another, and he rode a horse to school every day.

The other impression I have from novels about English boarding schools is that they're institutions committed to shaping the character of their students. It seems you can actually tell where someone went to school by how they talk and "carry themselves." As you know from the years you spent living here, American schools are vastly different. Your schools are explicitly engaged in the project of producing certain kinds of people. It's sometimes said that England won this or that war on the playing fields of Eton. If that's true, it's both a good thing and a bad thing, but even if it's done badly, at least someone's trying.

I make these rambling remarks because I think being in a boarding school means that you're confronting a reality that up until now you may not have anticipated: many of your schoolmates will find your family's robust commitment to the Christian faith to be distinctly odd, if not perverse. By attending such a school and living away from your parents, you'll discover how odd it is that you're a Christian. You'll make friends with fellow students who've never given a second thought to being Christian. Yet you're a person whose mother has recently become a bishop. Your fate, I fear, is set. Being a Christian or not being a Christian will always be extremely significant for you. Because you're approaching the time in your life when you'll have to ask yourself what being a Christian means, in this letter I want to direct your attention to the virtue of faith.

You're growing up, becoming a young man, so you'll begin to face challenges that you may not have imagined. One of those challenges will be how you negotiate your life as a Christian. There are virtues peculiar to the Christian tradition—the virtues of hope, faith, and charity. I've already commended hope and charity, but now I think it's time to consider faith.

Oddly enough, that faith is the subject of this letter is probably due more to cats than the worries I've sketched above. Last year I wrote to you about the death of our cat Eden, so you know that Paula and I are great lovers of cats—in particular, Siamese cats. Tuck, the cat I brought to our marriage, lived to be twenty-two. But as soon as Paula was in his life, he chose to be her cat. His death made us very sad, but after a period of mourning, we bought two kittens. We named the female Eden and the male Enda. Last year Enda died not long after Eden. They were both eighteen years old. Their deaths also made us very sad because we loved them and cherished their distinctive personalities.

We waited about six months after they had died before bringing new kittens into our lives. Then we found two female Siamese kittens that were two months old when we brought them home. We named them Faith and Hope. Kittens, of course, are into everything, and Faith and Hope were—and still are—into everything. They're a joy to watch. They play endlessly with one another, but because they're Siamese, they're also very people-oriented. We've already fallen in love with them.

I confess I'm a bit hesitant to mention the cats in this letter, given my account of Eden's death last year. It may give you the impression that cats matter to me more than they should. I do enjoy the cats, but I call your attention to them here because of their names. I'm sure one of the reasons I'm commending faith to you is that almost every day now I have reason to use the word "faith." It's "Faith, come here" or

"Faith, don't do that." So Faith is an everyday reality in my life in a way not unlike the way faith has been an everyday reality in your life. Being a Christian in the Wells family simply comes with the drinking water. But now you've "gone out into a world" in which being a Christian isn't a given. And you'll discover it's a lifelong task to say why you follow Christ.

Many Christians think what makes them Christian is to say they have faith in God. There are good reasons to express it that way, but in the world in which we find ourselves, to put it in these terms can be misleading because it makes "faith" a form of "belief." As a result, being a Christian seems to be a matter of holding a set of propositions about God. And many draw the implication that what it means to be a Christian is to believe twenty-six impossible things before breakfast.

It's certainly true that faith has something to do with believing that the God we worship is a very particular God who has done some very peculiar things—"I have chosen you, Israel, to be my promised people"—but faith isn't first and foremost about holding a set of beliefs. No, faith is first and foremost a virtue. And it's a virtue made possible by being members of a community called church. That community habituates us in a way that makes us people who can be trusted. That we can be trusted

Faith isn't first and foremost about holding a set of beliefs. No, faith is first and foremost a virtue. And it's a virtue made possible by being members of a community called church.

shouldn't be surprising if we remember that the church is made up of people who think they should keep their promises. Deep connections bind trust and faith.

Unfortunately, some Christians think that what we believe can't be "proven," so faith is thought necessary because "everyone has to believe in something." But faith isn't the determined stance in the face of negative evidence to "believe that God exists." Faith is the acknowledgment that the God who called Abraham out of his home can be trusted to be true to the promises he made. In that respect, faith is more like the expectation I have when I come home at the end of the day. I can count on Faith to welcome me. I don't *try* to believe she'll do it: I *know* she'll do it. Similarly, Christians don't have to try to believe X or Y. But they discover that they do believe, for instance, that Jesus rose from the dead because they couldn't make sense of their lives otherwise.

In the fourth chapter of Paul's letter to the Romans, Paul argues that God didn't render Abraham righteous because he was a person of great moral integrity. And Paul also points out that the law couldn't make Abraham righteous because the law hadn't yet been given. Instead, Abraham's righteousness was possible only because God's grace makes faith possible. That's why faith is best understood as our being taken up into God's refusal to let our sin determine his relation to us. It does little good to believe that God exists if doing so doesn't make it possible for us to leave our homes to discover ourselves as God's people on the journey.

God not only promised Abraham the land of Canaan; Abraham was also told he would be the father of a numerous people. At this point Abraham and his wife, Sarah, were old, well beyond child-bearing years. Yet Paul praises Abraham because "no distrust made him waver concerning the promise of God, but he grew strong in his faith as he gave glory to God, being fully convinced that God was able to do what he had promised. Therefore his faith was 'reckoned to him as righteousness'" (Rom. 4:20–22). Faith, then, is a matter of trust in a God who steadfastly cares for his people.

But I need to be candid with you and acknowledge that I seldom use the word "faith" in speech or writing. I don't use it because, as I've suggested, I try to resist the presumption that "faith" is an epistemological concept. I'm aware, of course, that "epistemology" is a word beyond your current pay grade, but it simply means the attempt to understand the words that make our world our world. Rather than write about faith, I tend to use the word "faithful." I do so because our "faithfulness" can and must be construed as an attempt to be followers of Jesus. Jesus invites us to come and be his disciples by faithfully following his lead. That means faith and discipleship are interdependent.

> *Jesus invites us to come and be his disciples by faithfully following his lead. That means faith and discipleship are interdependent.*

Though it's difficult to know for sure, I suspect that faith became an epistemological category during the Reformation. Protestants alleged that Catholics believed that works were necessary if we were to be made righteous, but Martin Luther insisted that it's only by the grace of God that we are made perfect by faith. This produced the famous "law" of the Reformation—that we are saved by the grace of God, not by works. That's why Protestants accused Catholics of "works righteousness"—because Catholics allegedly thought good deeds were necessary for our salvation. I gladly report to you that the polemics surrounding these Reformation issues are increasingly seen as false alternatives. Righteousness isn't a matter of faith and works; it's a matter of whether we're faithful followers of Christ.

Which finally brings me back to the world you're confronting in boarding school. Not too long ago, to be English and to be Christian were assumed to be pretty much the same thing. To "be of the Christian faith" suggested a status rather than a virtue that was the result of habits acquired by undertaking an arduous task or journey. You didn't need to be on a journey because it was assumed you had arrived. Happily, that world, the world in which being English and being Christian were assumed to be equivalent, is now gone. So to be the son of a mother who's a bishop means you had better have faith in God because, in no doubt very different ways, God has found a way to make your life odd. I think you'll discover that to be odd and to be a person of faith may be different ways of saying "I'm a Christian." But I think you'll find nothing is more important than your ability to say "I have faith in God, the Father of our Lord, Jesus Christ, through the work of the Holy Spirit."

Peace and love,

Stan

Character

≈ *January 31, 2017* ≈

Dear Laurie,

This letter is different. I'm not writing on the anniversary of your baptism, nor am I writing only to you. I'm writing with the knowledge that these letters will be published and I hope widely read. Still, I hope that you'll find these last reflections on the nature of the moral life useful. You're close to being "grown up" now. I'm not sure what it means to be "grown up"—I'm seventy-six and I still keep wondering if I'm there. But I think that being a person of character at least means you're becoming who you've been called to be. In short, you're discovering how important character is for living well.

I've spent a lifetime trying to convince those who think about ethics that character and the virtues are crucial for any adequate account of what it means to

live well. Of course, character and the virtues are
manifest in the decisions
and choices we make, but
the *kind* of decisions and
choices we make are de-
termined by our character.

*Character and the
virtues are crucial
for any adequate
account of what it
means to live well.*

I think it's true, as the writer Iris Murdoch main-
tained, that decisions are what we make when everything else has been lost. She wasn't denying that we
all make decisions, but for people of character, the
decisions made don't seem to be decisions because
these individuals, given their character, given who
they are, assume they could have done nothing other
than what they have done.

This seems straightforward enough, but there are
a number of conceptual problems raised by the introduction of character into this book that shouldn't
be overlooked. Not the least problem is the embarrassing fact that it is by no means clear that we know
what we're talking about when we praise someone
for having character. For one thing, character isn't
simply the sum of the virtues, because it isn't clear
that there *is* a sum of the virtues.

For another thing, the virtues are instilled in us
by our acting in a specific way. Aristotle's way of
putting the matter is that the virtues develop from

corresponding activities. That seems straightforward, but it's tricky because of the ambiguity contained in the word "corresponding." Yet it's still true that the virtues are habits acquired through training in practices and activities that make up a way of life. But character doesn't seem to be a correlative of any single activity or form of life. Rather, character seems to be the general orientation of a person, an orientation that is quite mysterious because we aren't sure of its source. And some people seem to have it, while others don't.

Aristotle does believe that the various virtues must finally be united, but he doesn't seem to think that character is a name for that unity. It's not even clear if we ever achieve such unity in this life. Yet the virtues must be enacted in the way a person of character would enact them. This seems to suggest, as is often the case in Aristotle, a circular argument that isn't necessarily vicious. But it does leave many questions without clear answers.

You can feel Aristotle struggling with these questions surrounding character when he suggests that people of character have a "natural gift of vision" which enables them to have lives determined by the good. But to have this gift doesn't mean we're not responsible for our character, even though, as Aristotle puts it, our character is the result of "particular steps" that are "imperceptible." Clearly Aristotle comes close to suggesting that those who have a good character are just lucky.

In light of these considerations, it's interesting to note that a bad person may in spite of themselves be a person of character. That way of putting the matter doesn't seem quite right because it suggests that a person can be distinguished from their character. Yet don't we often say that a person has a bad character? I'm not quite sure how to straighten these things out, but they show that what it means to have character is by no means a simple matter.

Aristotle worries that some may conclude that, given the ambiguities surrounding character, we're not responsible for being people of character. But he argues that the unjust or self-indulgent person at one time could have chosen not to be this way. For that reason, they're responsible for having acquired these traits voluntarily. Once these traits are acquired, Aristotle concludes, the unjust or self-indulgent person can no longer be anything other than what they are.

This last sentence suggests, understandably but wrongly, that character may be just another word for what we now call "personality." We associate an individual's personality with such descriptors as extroverted or introverted, kind or calculating, self-giving or self-involved, generous or stingy, happy or unhappy. The list could go on indefinitely and be as various as the different cultures that shape us. What to do with such a list? If character names the kind of person we are, then character may share some of the traits we associate with personality. But that doesn't mean that character is just another word for personality, because character seems to require a self-knowledge that personality doesn't.

Still, it may be the case that character and personality aren't independent of one another. For example, we often describe someone as "quite some character," or we say of someone, "What a character!" Those phrases suggest, though not always in a complimentary way, that someone is quite distinctive. And someone who's "quite a character" may or may not be a person of character. This suggests that having a good character is a much more serious business than being a character.

> *Someone who's "quite a character" may or may not be a person of character. This suggests that having a good character is a much more serious business than being a character.*

Yet I think the association of character and personality rightly suggests that a person of character is someone who's distinctive. Perhaps another way to put it is that they have a certain "style." To have style is to be a person who has cultivated a way of life for which they owe no one other than themselves an explanation. In other words, to have style is to be self-assured that I am who I seem to be. This is the kind of knowledge that defines people of character, and that's why they can be called on to act in certain ways that are expected of them, given who they are.

Your father suggested a way to think about character that I find quite compatible with what I've been struggling to say. Character, he says, is who we are when no one's looking. Character so conceived suggests that a person of character is happy with who they are so they don't have to try to be someone they're not. Whether alone or with others, they're the same person. Through the contingencies that constitute all lives, they have a life narrative that they believe makes them who they are. That's what it means to be a person of character.

That character requires or makes possible a self-knowledge otherwise unavailable is a crucial insight if we're to understand the role that character plays in the acquisition of the virtues. People of good character know themselves in a way that makes possible a frank and honest appraisal of themselves. This kind of self-knowledge is just a correlative of their interactions with others. They are, quite simply, people we enjoy being with.

Though character is a richer concept than personality, it is still true that there are similarities between the two. Both suggest that there is something distinctive about each person, which makes, for example, how one person acquires courage and practices it different from how another person does so. Character and the virtues that character shapes reflect the contingent character of our lives, which means we discover who we are through the retrospective judgments that character makes possible. In other words, we think our lives are lived facing forward, but looking back is crucial for the virtuous life because it requires us to make judgments about whether we have acted well and, on that basis, whether certain actions should be repeated or corrected in the future.

As I've mentioned before, Alasdair MacIntyre suggests, in his book *After Virtue,* that Jane Austen created or discovered a virtue that hadn't been named before she called our attention to it: the virtue of constancy. Austen associated this virtue with the kind of life characteristic of English sea captains, because her brother was one. It may be that the naming of constancy hadn't been necessary before because people understood that to be a person of character one had to be courageous in a way that a person of patience must be. I call attention to constancy because it seems quite close to what character entails. To have character is to be a person of constancy. All of which may just be a way to say that if you're a person of character, you're someone who can be trusted.

> *I call attention to constancy because it seems quite close to what character entails. To have character is to be a person of constancy. All of which may just be a way to say that if you're a person of character, you're someone who can be trusted.*

Recently, David Brooks, who is a popular writer about culture and politics in *The New York Times*, wrote a book called *The Road to Character*. I think it's quite a good book. He's not a philosopher, but he has good philosophical instincts. For example, he doesn't try—as I've just tried—to get a conceptual hold on what he means by character. Instead, his book is made up of brief biographies of people he believes displayed character in their lives. He's chosen people like Dwight Eisenhower, George Marshall, George Eliot, and Frances Perkins. His portraits of them might be thought of as character studies. While you might want to disagree with his account of one or another of those he commends, his fundamental intuition strikes me as sound. By this I mean that he assumes the best way to get at what character is about is through exemplification.

There's a basic argument that shapes Brooks's choice of those he holds up as people of character. He suggests that there are two kinds of virtues that currently shape our lives—résumé virtues and eulogy virtues. Résumé virtues are those like efficiency and time management that are valued by the marketplace. Eulogy virtues are those he identifies as aspects of character that others praise in you when you're not present. Humility, kindness, and courage are examples of eulogy virtues. Eulogies are, of course, a genre of funeral orations, which means I need to say something about death.

Character is finally that determined orientation that gives us lives worth living in the face of death. As I've suggested, character entails having self-knowledge that allows us to make our lives our own. Such knowledge takes the form of a narrative that aids us in connecting the contingencies of our lives in a way that helps us make sense of what often seems to be just a jumble.

> *Character entails having self-knowledge that allows us to make our lives our own.*

As Christians, we believe such a narrative is to be found in God's care and love of us through the calling of Israel and the life, death, and resurrection of Christ. We know we're going to die, which may seem to render pointless a life of virtue and character, but as Christians we can imagine no other alternative. Self-knowledge for Christians also means having the resources—and resources is just another word for friends—to recognize when we're living lives that are inconsistent with being followers of Christ.

It's not clear to me that Brooks quite understood the significance of classifying the virtues according to the distinction between résumé virtues and eulogy virtues. Often it's quite difficult even at funerals to give a positive account of a person's life because it seems to have gone wrong and never recovered. Such lives happen, and often they're not thought to be problematic because they've been so full of the résumé virtues. But Christians celebrate lives that haven't flourished according to the standards of the résumé virtues, doing so because those who have lived them have, for example, been generous even when they've had very little. Christians can celebrate these lives because we know we haven't been called into existence to be successful. Instead, we've been born to praise the Lord, which, interestingly enough, makes us content with the lives we've been given. We can see this by taking a look at Christian history. Throughout the centuries, Christians, even in the midst of suffering for the faith, still found they wouldn't want to have any lives other than the ones they'd been given.

Paul, in his letter to the Romans, gets this just right. He's in prison, which he doesn't seem to regret. Instead, he claims to boast in his suffering because "suffering produces endurance, and endurance produces character, and character produces hope, and hope does not disappoint us, because God's love has been poured into our hearts through the Holy Spirit that has been given to us" (Rom. 5:3–5).

I'm going to miss writing these letters to you because they make me think about matters that I believe matter. I'm aware that this last letter may betray my attempt to write to you in such a way that I could connect with who you were at the time. I suspect I wasn't very successful in that endeavor in previous letters, although I certainly tried. I'm sure I don't know the challenges you face on a daily basis, and I'm clueless about what people call popular culture.

But, before I end this letter, this book, there's one development in our culture and politics I must mention. It seems that we've entered a time in which truth no longer matters in our public life and politics. And people of character like you are going to find that this is a difficult world to negotiate. I have just one simple recommendation for how you must live in such a world: Don't lie.

You may well wonder if that's all I have to say. Not to lie doesn't even sound like a virtue. Further complicating matters is the fact that most people think that lying is wrong, yet this general agreement masks our confusion about what constitutes a lie, as is clear from recent events in American life. Lying may be rightly understood as intentionally saying what we know to be false in order to deceive, but it turns out that we're often unsure about what's true. Thus the Austrian-British philosopher Ludwig Wittgenstein remarks in his book *Culture and Value* that "the truth can be spoken only by someone who is already at home in it, not by someone who lives in untruthfulness, and does no more than reach out toward it from within untruthfulness."

I hope that the accounts of the virtues in these letters will help you be at home in the truth, which is no easy accomplishment. We often "shade the truth" because we fear losing the love or regard of those who mean much to us. To be at home in the truth is also a demanding business because so often we lie first and foremost to ourselves, since we fear facing what we can only acknowledge as a failure. In short, we lie to ourselves and others not because we're corrupt but because we want to be good.

The temptation will be to seek a theory of truth in order to avoid lying. But that's precisely what many think we no longer have. This isn't a new problem. We are representatives of a tradition that has at its center the One who we believe not only was at home in the truth but was and is the truth. When a minor Roman official was told that this man was the one who had come into the world to testify to the truth, he asked the skeptic's question: "What is truth?" He received no answer. The ensuing silence indicated that the response to skepticism is not a theory but an exemplary life. Such a life, a life that is at home in the truth, is, according to Wittgenstein, a life that has undergone the training to keep pride in check.

I believe that you've been put on the path to becoming at home in the truth. Never take that for granted. Living in the truth may give you a life that's difficult, but it will be one that will make it possible for you to look back and want no other life than the one you've lived. As my friend and your father Sam Wells suggests, the only things that will last are those things that embody the truth. To have such a life will not only serve you well, but also your neighbor, who, given the times in which we live, may feel completely lost. So don't lie. You'll need all the virtues I've recommended—and more—to be at home in the truth. It will be hard, I know, and it may involve suffering, but as we've learned from Paul, suffering produces endurance, and endurance produces character, and character produces hope, and hope does not disappoint us. May that be your watchword always.

Peace and love,

Stan